THE NEW AGE
IN A NUTSHELL

A Guide to Living in New Times

Lorna St. Aubyn

Foreword by David Lorimer

Gateway Books, Bath

First published in 1990
by GATEWAY BOOKS
The Hollies, Wellow,
Bath, BA2 8QJ

© *1990 Lorna St. Aubyn*

Setting in 11 / 12.5 pt Sabon
by Photosetting & Secretarial Services, Yeovil
Printed & bound by
Wheaton of Exeter
Cover design by Vanessa Kelly

British Libary Cataloguing in Publication Data
St. Aubyn, Lorna, 1929-
  The new age in a nutshell; a guide to living in new
  times.
  1. Man. Nature – Anthroposophical viewpoints
  I. Title
  133

ISBN 0 946551 58 8

Awake, awake, the world is young
For all its weary years of thought.
The starkest fights must not be fought,
The most surprising songs be sung

James Elroy Fletcher

Table of Contents

Foreword

Even the most die-hard conservative cannot help noticing that we are living through a period of dramatic change, not to say upheaval in many spheres of our lives. We are affected socially, economically, mentally, emotionally and spiritually. Our health and immune systems are in precarious balance: people are facing the kind of breakdowns which call for a radical reassessment of life purpose and direction. There is increasing doubt that the materialist world picture is telling us the whole truth, with its insistence on a meaningless universe, human life as a cosmic accident, and consciousness as a by-product of brain processes: we therefore perish as individuals at death.

So Life asks us to consider the crucial questions concerning our identity and purpose; we become conscious explorers. But what next? Where do we turn when we hear such terms as ecological awareness, the Age of Aquarius, earth energies, karma, reincarnation, chakras etc.? What does it all mean? Does it amount to a coherent world picture? To say that the New Age offers a cogent philosophy of life would be an exaggeration, but it is true to say that there is a great deal of teaching on offer which shares a few basic principles.

It is the object of this 'Nutshell' to provide the reader with a critical introduction to the New Age 'scene'. I stress the important word 'critical', since there is a great deal of credulity and gullibility abroad, a lack of discrimination which stems partly from a mistrust of the 'head' (especially so-called left-brain rationalism) by the 'heart'. It should be obvious that head and heart are to be integrated, without, of course forgetting the will which puts it all into practice.

The first part of this book surveys some of the major principles of the New Age world picture, and therefore challenges the philosophical assumptions of scientific rationalism by suggesting that we all have a subtle anatomy of chakras, that our essential self is recincarnated and is responsible for its actions, and that the Earth is a living energy system with which we can enter into conscious relationship. Suffering and loss are shown to play an educative role in life: they are not to be avoided or shunned on the grounds of some naive utilitarianism by claiming that the pleasure principle is the basis of our life experience.

Part Two is more personal, probing how a new understanding of one's life and attitudes directly. If life is a learning process, then there are all kinds of lessons, pleasant and unpleasant, programmed into the curriculum. The key questions in any situation are what one can learn from it, and how one has helped bring it about; this last remark reflects another New Age assumption that nothing is entirely accidental, that we shape our own reality with the patterns of our minds: if we change our minds ("metanoia"), we change our lives. This book will be a great help to those who need an introduction to New Age thinking; it will give them an expanded and meaningful picture of themselves, life and the world about us, enabling them to give a new direction to their lives.

David Lorimer,
Hampnett, March 1990.

Introduction to Part One

Gradually, more and more people are becoming interested in the new way of life that could emerge for the Aquarian Age. Based on the essence of teachings common to many epochs and cultures, but adapted for a world that has changed drastically, this New Age thinking proposes an entirely different attitude towards ourselves, the earth, and all aspects of our life while on this planet. Because the threads of so many different traditions are being drawn together to form this picture, there is a bewildering glut of teaching on offer. By presenting a brief over-view of the principles common to Aquarian thinking, this book will attempt to make of them a coherent whole. It will also make clear the immense amount of change which must come about if we are successfully to manoeuvre our way through the coming 2000 years.

Because the paths by which newcomers can first approach this thinking are so diverse, it is important that we choose the one that is easiest and most natural to us. Whether we are attracted by the way of the scientist or the mystic, that of the earth-lover or the intellectual, will depend largely on our education and the qualities of our mind and temperament. If later on we become aware of former lives, we may well find that these present preferences stem from centuries of past training. If, for instance, someone has studied healing in its many forms over several lifetimes, it will almost certainly be via the path of the healer that he approaches the New Age. Someone, on the other hand, who has experienced many incarnations in a convent, monastery or temple will be drawn to

1

this new philosophy of life by all that the mystics have contributed to it.

The ideas discussed in this book have never been part of the popular or accessible culture. In early times esoteric spiritual teachings, often known as the Ancient Wisdom or the Perennial Philosophy, were in the hands of small groups of Initiates who had undergone very specific formal training. It was those who had attained the highest stage of spiritual understanding who carefully passed on this knowledge from one generation to the next - often in code. These teachings were considered to be such dynamite to the uninitiated, that the penalty for revealing them was death.

During the very early years of Christianity, a much greater participation in the life of the spirit than hitherto been allowed to the masses appears to have been considered admissible. Although Jesus clearly indicated that people must be taught by different means according to their state of evolution (the Parables, for instance, contain teaching on many different levels), the fact that He promised all of us direct access to God through Himself gives us a hint as to the vast leap forward He had hoped to achieve for mankind by incarnating. But, sadly, with the founding of the Church, politics and power very quickly became dominant preoccupations of its authorities. Not wanting this power in any way challenged, they denied the validity of the ancient wisdom, which from then on played no part in Church doctrine and was driven underground. The Spiritual Law and empirical mysticism once taught in the temples became matters for the secret brotherhoods and sisterhoods, whose beneficial influence on the world could be expressed only indirectly.

Over the past 400 years the situation changed. With the development of science and the rational faculties of man, the authority of traditional religion lessened and that of rationalism, in the form of science, grew. The danger to the ancient esoteric traditions shifted. They were no longer being persecuted by the Inquisition but mocked by Science. Again they had to stay hidden. Then suddenly, as the Aquarian Age first stirred at the end of the 19th century, a whole spate of esoteric teachings suddenly became openly available. Heralded by Madame Blavatsky and the Theosophists, they were quickly followed by Rudolf Steiner, Gurdjieff and Ouspensky. The hidden teachings of the Essenes were made known by Szekely; the secrets of the Hunas were unveiled by the American, Max Freedom Long. Clearly the necessity for secrecy had been outgrown. The Aquarian Age, whose keynote is self-responsibility, demands that mankind now be given the opportunity of choice and self-determination, even if our new-found knowledge and power prove to be our undoing.

What this promises is a very exciting advance in man's evolution. The search for meaning is one of our basic needs in life but, while the golden thread of true spiritual teaching has been given since the dawn of culture, those who wish power over others (the left hand path) have also sought to take advantage of people's search for spiritual development. Seeking always to enslave mankind for their own purposes, they super-cunningly present themselves as teachers of self-empowerment. For them this could be a great heyday, for they thrive on illusion and self-inflation. Stringent discrimination is the best weapon against them. A hypersensitive touchstone by which to recognize the motives and quality all teachers must be developed in each of us. Being open to this wealth of fascinating knowledge, each strand of which can weave itself into our understanding of the whole, is excellent as long as we are constantly sorting and assessing what we absorb.

The same caution applies to all information now being so freely diffused through 'channels' or mediums, parapsychological research, or past life recalls. The higher worlds, only too anxious to help us at this very difficult time, are doing their best to raise our awareness by all possible means. But at the same time, like many of the more sober New Age teachers, they are begging us to beware. Beginners should, they say, seek guidance from someone with more experience; basic groundwork must be done before seeking to assimilate advanced knowledge. Great dangers lie in the topsyturvy, haphazard mode of learning that has replaced the rigid structures of the old Mystery Schools. Somehow a happy compromise must be found between the openness and caution.

With the raising of consciousness of a large number of people –
who must logically constitute the first wave of New Age students
– more trust can now be put in the spiritual law of attraction: they
will be drawn to study what they need to know and what they can
cope with. It is frequently reported by new seekers that their
learning seems to be guided by something beyond their logical
mind. The book most useful to them almost 'fell off' the shelf at
their feet; the seminar most valid for them was the one for which
they had both time and money.

Another law will also be helping to protect us if we have already
played our part in the process by exercising as much discrimination
as we can. Like the principle of attraction, it goes beyond logic and
was said to be a basic factor in the Temple teaching methods. There
it was a common practice for neophytes to begin their studies by
learning by heart the entire wisdom of the Temple, which was
inscribed on a series of columns. *Consciously* they retained of all
that knowledge only that which was relevant to their first months
of study. As they advanced, they slowly brought into their conscious mind what they had learned parrot-fashion earlier, but were
only now able to understand.

The handing down of the Ancient Wisdom by generations of
initiates, has in the past been fraught with danger because of both
persecution and the wilful or involuntary destruction of the precious records kept on stones and crystals and in holy sites. Now our
methods of keeping alive this knowledge are clearly changing. That
teaching having moved from the enclosed orders into the market
place has advantages despite its dangers. With modern research
able to re-discover so much that has been lost, and modern record-
ing methods able to make the discoveries safe for the future, we
have hopefully found a reliable means of keeping alive the ancient
tradition, without which we would indeed be impoverished.

In order for our passage into the Aquarian Age to be safely
negotiated, man must become whole again, and the balance
between himself and the earth be restored. Despite the many
prophecies of doom all around us, this could happen. In an
unprecedented state of agreement, the seers, astrologers and a few

pioneering voices of science assert that a great quantum leap in consciousness is imminent. Evolution, we are now told, does not progress steadily as we once thought; it happens in a series of infrequent forward bounds, of which the one now being anticipated is greater than any yet experienced by mankind. If we can avoid the self-destruction on which we appear so bent, and if each of us pledges our active participation in the changes, we have before us a time which promises to be highly rewarding.

The author would like at this point to reassure her readers that although she has used 'he' and 'man' throughout this book when referring to the collective human being, it has been done in the interest of non-clumsy English, NOT because of any intended slight towards womankind.

1

The Zodiacal Ages

The Aquarian Age is a term commonly used but seldom related to the overall concept of which it is part. In order to understand the significance of the transition we are now making from the Piscean Age into that of Aquarius, it could be helpful to consider briefly the basic structures of astrology and to survey the zodiacal ages since the beginning of conventionally recorded history.

During a calendar year, the sign of the Zodiac changes monthly; in the larger cycles of 'Ages', each one lasts approximately 2160 years. In both cases the transition periods at the beginning and end of the month or age are times when characteristics of both the outgoing and the in-coming signs exert an attenuated influence. Because of this mingling of very disparate energies and values, all change-over periods from one age to another are invariably accompanied by great upheavals. The overthrowing of old traditions and religions and the establishment of new social structures are the outward manifestations of all the unrest and change occurring at a deep level.

Our first tentative steps into the Aquarian Age were taken in the 1880's. On the material/scientific plane great advances were suddenly made, especially in realms appropriate to an air, thinking-oriented sign, as is Aquarius. Flying machines were invented; communication by telephone and telegraph became possible. In the intellectual/spiritual field there appeared with Madame Blavatsky and the Theosophists the first of a series of teachings which were to spread in the next hundred years all over the world, forming the basis of what has grown into New Age thought. With the birth of spiritualism, the way was prepared for the realization, so long suppressed, that consciousness is not extinguished by physical death. Out of these first proofs of survival could emerge the conviction now spreading that all souls have a long and arduous journey between the time that they leave the Godhead and return to it, and that at all times during that journey, whether incarnate or discarnate, they are in some state of consciousness. The process of entering the Aquarian Age has now been well and truly engaged, but it will take a few more decades before the world can really benefit from the Aquarian energies, and the influences of the chaotic transition period die out.

Each sign of the Zodiac manifests certain characteristics which are reflected in those people born under its influence. The zodiacal ages function similarly, except that it is now the world rather than individuals which reflects the characteristics of the sign. We can expect then to see all areas of man's activities, architecture, agriculture, science, travel, human relationships etc., profoundly affected by the values and ideals of Aquarius, as previous ages have been by their signs.

Because the ages follow each other in the reverse order to that of the months' progression, the age of Leo (10,800 B.C. – 8,640 B.C.) was followed by the Cancerian Age, then the Taurean, then the age of Aries, the Piscean and now the Aquarian. During the age of Leo, the main centre of civilization lay in the Andes, where many Atlanteans had taken refuge when they realized that part of their continent would soon be destroyed. This South American civilization took as its symbols the lion, statues of which are a prominent feature in its temple remains, and the sun, said to be ruled by the sign of Leo. The force within the sun (not the sun itself, as is sometimes alleged), was worshipped. It was a passionate and dramatic time, its deity a fiery, masculine one. The colour gold personified it: not only was physical gold widely used, it was also said to be a Golden Age during which man lived in close harmony with himself and his planet.

With the advent of the age of Cancer (8,640 B.C. – 6,480 B.C.), the

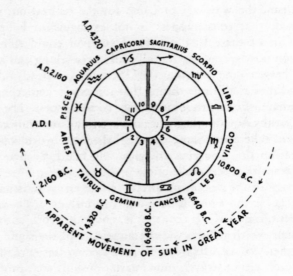

	Age	Dominant Sign	Ruling Planet	Opposite Sign
Circa	B.C. 10800-8640	LEO	SUN	AQUARIUS
,,	B.C. 8640-6430	CANCER	MOON	CAPRICORN
,,	B.C. 6430-4320	GEMINI	MERCURY	SAGITTARIUS
,,	B.C. 4320-2160	TAURUS	VENUS	SCORPIO
,,	B.C. 2160-A.D. 1	ARIES	MARS	LIBRA
,,	A.D. 1-2160	PISCES	JUPITER	VIRGO
,,	A.D. 2160-4320	AQUARIUS	SATURN AND URANUS	LEO

The Zodiacal Ages

emphasis in the world changed to a feminine, lunar one. The Moon goddess reigned supreme, and it was women who played the key roles both in government and religion. Cancer being a water sign and the Moon being the mistress of magic, the civilizations which flourished then were less flamboyant, more mystical and introverted. After the powerful, courageous spiritual impulse generated in mankind by the age of Leo, it was now the emotional and psychic faculties which were given space in which to develop. In the passing of the seed from the Father to the Mother, these new moon-cults were the logical polarity to the earlier sun worship. It was a time when fertility was emphasized and the family was the central focus of society. The main sites of these civilizations were in Asia Minor and along the shores of the Mediterranean. The early cultures of Japan and China were also deeply influenced by Cancerian ideals.

The principle of duality was born in the age of Gemini (6,840 B.C. – 4,320 B.C.), whose symbol is the twins, offspring of the Father-Mother God. Intellectual and ingenious, as befits the children of an air sign, they introduced into both social and religious life the need to classify and communicate. It was during this age that the first alphabets were invented and that discoveries began to be recorded. Great artistic advances were also made. The Godhead, which had until then been extremely remote, now became for the first time humanized. It was in Greece, early Egypt, the Euphrates and Assyria that the main civilizations prospered during the Age of Gemini.

The great flowering of Egypt occurred during the Taurean Age (4,320 B.C. – 2,160 B.C.). Founded earlier by another group of Atlanteans, their attention was focussed during this age on two principal preoccupations of the earth sign Taurus: those of material security and building. This is the epoch which produced the Pyramids and some of the greatest temples ever created by mankind. Solid, enduring qualities were valued. Worship of the bull – symbol of Taurus – was a strong feature in their religion, which sought always to ground the Divine. With its emphasis on the enjoyment of all earthly beauty and bounty, the Taurean Age manifested a quite different aspect of the feminine from that of the Cancerian Mother Goddesses.

By the time the world moved into the age of Aries, (2,160 B.C. – 1 A.D.), a masculine fire impetus was again predominant, but the characteristics of Aries being very different from those of Leo, the civilizations which developed under its influence had a quite different flavour to those of the earlier South American cultures. As the first sign in the Zodiac, Aries is young and impetuous. The civilizations that arose during those two millenia were very vital, many of them nomadic, as though the life force they expressed were too great to be contained by walls. Its symbol is the ram, which so well denotes that headlong battering quality which made that Age one of conquest and exploration. Heroic man, encouraged to reach always higher, was their ideal. Their mythology was heavily preoccupied with the meeting of the human with the divine. It was a time of prophetic vision and idealism when a monotheistic concept of God was first put into practice.

As in all transitions from one age to another, preparation for the Piscean Age (which began with the birth of Jesus), was made gradually during the last hundred years of Aries' reign, in this case by sects such as the Essenes. The water sign of Pisces has as one of its main symbols a fish, which was used by the early Christians as a sign of recognition. Of all the three water signs, Pisces is the most emotional, and it was this characteristic which dominated the Christian era. It was a time when sacrifice was admired and emulated. Limitations were also deliberately imposed on oneself and others: the stern life of convents and monasteries became a powerful form of self-expression.

There is here an interesting contrast with the developing Aquarian Age when it is already clear that group life – the most important concern of Aquarius – will now take on quite different forms. The greater freedom of communes and community living is already replacing walled religious establishments. The search for self-responsibility, which is such a typical Aquarian trait, no longer allows us to hand over our lives to someone else's keeping, whatever the advantages. Whereas in a Piscean group the individual was subjected to the collective, at whatever cost to himself, in an Aquarian group the individual is allowed far more voice. How institutions such as the army will adapt to this new trend is very interesting. Already its old unquestioning discipline has been challenged since Vietnam. But because of the emphasis we can expect in the coming millenia on communal living and global unity, more co-operative working methods will no doubt soon develop in all spheres of life, even those which have been thought to need the most rigid structures.

The symbol of Aquarius is a man pouring water onto the earth. He is the individual who feeds the whole. This impersonal giving is then the next stage in humanity's development. In the same way that individuals pass each month through the influence of a new sign so that they learn new lessons, so does mankind pass cyclically through these long ages in order to confront and develop all aspects of its identity. The more aware we can be of the demands and gifts of Aquarius, the better we can help fulfill this crucial new cycle.

2

Reincarnation

Although the concept of reincarnation is far more complicated than it at first appears, and there are disparities in the teaching of its details, the important common assumption is that we return to earth hundreds of times in order to experience all that this planet has to teach us. Until perfection in earthly matters has been achieved, we are not freed from the need to incarnate.

When we first embark on our earth cycle, we are not given any choice as to the time, place and circumstances in which it would be suitable for us to incarnate. Our work at that kindergarten stage is simply to make the best of the material given to us. Without the experience of other earth lives, no sensible choices could be made. But gradually, with much assistance from the spiritual helpers we encounter between lifetimes, we begin to choose for our coming incarnation those opportunities and difficulties most able to help us grow. As our awareness progresses and we become able to envisage each lifetime as part of our total evolution, we are allowed increasing choice. It is this which bestows upon us our true freedom: nothing has been imposed upon us. However painful or difficult our life, we had recognized it to be necessary and agreed to experience it at a time when we had far greater vision than we would subsequently have on earth.

When we have at last perfected our Earth learning, and the necessity for returning here has passed, we can still choose to incarnate if we have good reason for so doing. Commitment to a particularly important task could be such a reason. (In the chapter on Guidance, a further option is described for souls who have reached liberation from earth: instead of progressing on their own evolutionary journey, they can choose to continue helping the human race as discarnate teachers working through certain individuals or groups.)

When first studying the process of reincarnation, it appears to be a simple alternation between life and 'death', which is perceived as a period of rest and assimilation between earth lives. But further study reveals it as being far more subtle and complex. The question of soul groups, for instance, introduces the idea that our lives are closely interlocked with those of certain other people, and that although we work spiritually as individuals, it is with and through members of our soul group that some of our most intense learning experiences occur. This does not mean that an entire group incarnates simultaneously in the same place; we might meet only one or two of its members in certain lives. A proportion of the group (the number varying according to its evolution and the work it is currently performing), is always needed 'on the other side' in order to maintain a balance and to help make conscious any teaching its members may have temporarily forgotten or have deliberately set aside.

Due to the critical nature of our times, most spiritually aware groups are now exceptionally heavily represented on earth, where their physical presence is vital. In order to compensate for this imbalance, its discarnate members are receiving increased help from higher beings, which can in turn be communicated to earth because of the strong psychic links existing between group members.

In order to imagine the procedure by which communication is established between the spiritual world and incarnate groups, it is perhaps helpful to visualize an electricity grid. By means of this the spiritual power emanating from God is stepped down through a series of 'transformers', i.e. spiritual beings, so as to be received at strengths acceptable to either the most evolved human beings, the most novice groups of souls, or those in-between. Through progressive incarnations we are then seeking to raise the level of our spiritual consciousness so that it can receive ever-higher teaching.

Whether an individual can belong to more than one soul group is a matter about which teachings differ. It seems probable that it depends on the complexity of the soul's path. If someone is working on several major themes, he may well need to belong to several groups, some of which he will not contact during certain incarnations, whereas some could overlap during others. The composition and size of these groups will, of course, vary at different times, but once you have connected with one of them, you are part of it, whether incarnate or discarnate, until the end of your earth cycle. It is even possible that these associations continue beyond that time, so that when a soul progresses to further cycles of experience on other planets or other levels, it will again choose to be with those to whom it was closest on earth.

Although it is difficult from our level of perception to understand exactly how this works, it seems possible that these groups are in some mysterious way interdependent, and that as their level of awareness increases and they grow closer to the Godhead, they merge, each reinforcing the other one's power.

The fact that members of a group can share the learning of all its other members can perhaps be best illustrated by the image of an octopus. In its body is contained everything that each of them has experienced since their first incarnation; each tentacle represents one of the group members. When the many-armed octopus sends down to earth one or more of its tentacles, everything that happens to that tentacle during its earth life will be communicated back to the group through its body, thus expanding the learning of all its members, whether incarnate or discarnate. Sharing as they do this body of common experience, the empathy and telepathy between group members can be extremely enabling and empowering; so too can the love and trust between them.

The fact that one person can experience a particular aspect of life for his entire group considerably multiplies the speed of our learning and is therefore in concordance with the spiritual law of economy which always tries to prevent the waste of either time or opportunity. Until this is understood, there will continue to be difficulties around this phenomenon. If, for instance, several people recall the same life so vividly that they genuinely think of it as their own, they are not necessarily the victims of fantasy and self-delusion; they may well be tapping in to this pool of shared experience.

When considering the much-debated questions of how many times and at what intervals souls need to incarnate in order to complete their Earth cycle, it is interesting to speculate whether certain souls so love this planet that they want to be here as often as possible, even if some of their lives will include much pain, whereas others basically hate the entire experience of material living and come here only reluctantly – as seldom as is allowed. It would also be interesting to know whether the latter's reluctance manifests itself from the very beginning of their journey on earth, or is it the outcome of their experiences here.

The use of family relationships in our pattern of incarnations is another fascinating subject. Because they mould our life so dramatically from the earliest age, they are often our best teachers. (It should be remembered that the people with whom we incarnate as close family can also be members of our soul group. These may even have agreed to play a very difficult, outwardly even negative, role in order to help us learn a difficult lesson quickly.) The search for non-possessiveness, the responsible use of power, the granting of space to others, loyalty and solidarity, are amongst the many tests that can be most speedily explored within the tightly-knit, intense atmosphere of family life.

The re-forming of links with companions from past lifetimes is governed, like all spiritual happenings, by the law of economy which helped us plan our lives so that we meet again those to whom we are spiritually closest. Especially at a difficult time of transition such as now, it would be unthinkable that we waste the effort of many lifetimes learning to live and work successfully with some-one. All loving and creative relationships are vitally needed now. Those which have a bad history also need to be re-activated so that amends can be made and the way cleared for light to enter the relationship. So despite the unprecedented number of souls now incarnate, it is not fanciful to assert that we are being re-united with people previously known; it is, on the contrary, logical. The more consciously we follow our path, the more surely will we recognize and begin working with those whom we can best help and be helped by.

Many esoteric schools teach that the reason we do not normally remember previous incarnations is because this knowledge would be detrimental to our well-being. Our faults and mistakes of the past should not, they say, be in any way given energy, nor should our former sadnesses and feelings of guilt. The positive and happy things we might remember would not, in their view, compensate for the difficult and discouraging memories we would bring forward. For them, all attempts at inducing past-life recalls are both wrong and dangerous. They believe that the 'oblivion' into which we are normally born is a protective mechanism provided by higher beings, and that we intrude into it at our peril. Only spontaneous recalls are considered by them to be safe, the person's psyche and his guides having allowed this material to surface because they consider him ready to deal with it.

This subject is treated more in depth in a later chapter. For the moment, suffice it to say that there are undoubtedly many traps into which we can fall when trying to learn more about our own history. Although some serious practitioners are attempting to help their clients become more self-aware through knowledge of the past, a sensationalist, money-orientated vortex of glamour is also being created around regressions. Wishful thinking is being fed and total credulity not being discouraged.

During the past centuries, belief in reincarnation has been almost entirely confined to the Eastern religions; now it is being more widely understood in the West. Had reincarnation not once been a basic tenet of the Christian faith, it is hard to see why the Emperor Justinian at the fifth Ecumenical Council at Constantinople in 553 found it necessary to 'declare the belief anathema', thereby forbidding its propagation.

Because so many people at present incarnate in Christian countries have experienced lives when reincarnation was never questioned, it is quite natural and easy for them to return to this paradigm which they feel to be immensely broadening and deepening. Once they re-connect with the idea that they are an integral part of the planet rather than a casual visitor to it, they will no longer stand by and watch in silence the dreadful destruction being perpetrated on a home they have loved for so long. Deeply involved in its destiny, they will begin to fulfill their roles as droplets of the Divine.

3

Karma

Karma, the law of cause and effect, although a demanding principle, is also entirely just, and one fights or even complains against it in vain. That which we sow shall we reap. Every action contains within itself logical and inevitable consequences. Every emotion brings about certain reactions. For an epoch where self-responsibility is being sought, karma is the ideal underlying principle. No external justice is needed: it is within life itself that we will find that which we deserve.

A perfect example of this is given by the great American seer Edgar Cayce in one of his books. A university professor who was born with severely impaired sight, was discovered by Cayce to have once been the member of a South American tribe whose job it was to blind all enemies captured in battle. Had he chosen that role voluntarily, he would almost certainly have been born totally blind in this lifetime, because he would have had to redeem his former pleasure in inflicting pain as well as experiencing the distress and fear he had caused his victims. But because he had been ordered to do this work by the elders of the tribe, he now only needed to be partially blind in order to redeem the past.

During each lifetime we create both good and bad karma. When dealing with it in each new incarnation, there are three stages through which we must ultimately pass: the retributive, the redemptive and the transcendant. When working at the retributive stage we try to 'balance our books' as justly as possible. Our noses are to the grindstone, and the issues we are working on are inescapable. To ignore them will only mean that a comparable situation will re-present itself in a future life. Once we have passed beyond the need for retribution, we reach an area where there is more choice. We are no longer merely making good past mistakes and injustices, we are voluntarily helping to dispel existing dishar-monies or imbalances. As time does not exist in linear form on the spiritual planes, we can actually change the past and modify the future. The transcendant phase is reached when the backlog of personal issues has been dealt with and service becomes the prime concern. At all times, even in the transcendant stage, great care must be taken to try to avoid creating new destructive karma for the future at all levels: personal, group, national and planetary.

Group karma works on the same principle as personal karma but has more complex ramifications because each member's experi-ence affects the entire group. Helping members of our soul group deal with their karma is therefore just as important as dealing with our own. No individual's progress depends solely on his own behaviour, especially as a group advances only at the speed of its slowest member. To discover who constitutes our spiritual group is then a matter of urgency; a joint effort at redeeming and ultimately transcending the group's karma will multiply the results obtained, the whole being far greater than the sum of its parts.

The question of national karma is an interesting one about which very little research has been done (the works of Rudolf Steiner probably give the greatest amount of information available on this subject). As a general principle, there would seem to be certain countries and races that have agreed to be used in order to expiate specific issues or to accomplish certain tasks. Poland could be seen as illustrating this very clearly. For several centuries she has been used as the lightning conductor of Eastern Europe, helping to contain through her own suffering the potential for wider confla-grations. Such excesses of persecution and occupation, imprison-ment and exile as have been borne by the Poles can only make a modicum of sense if seen as a corporate act of redemption. That they were one of the countries most affected by the Chernobyl disaster seems to confirm this pattern. It is impossible to postulate the exact mechanism at work here, but perhaps one can see this self-sacrifice of a nation as the equivalent of an individual's life of total service.

Interpreting planetary karma would require an even greater overview, but assuming that it works on the same principle as personal and group karma, it too must be transmuting its negativity in order to proceed with its evolution. As one small cog in the universe, our planet's role is as distinctive and vital as that of each individual working for mankind.

A clue about this specific role is given to us in the esoteric teaching which states that Earth is the planet of healing, the place where the entire cycle of healing can be learned and must be made manifest. Until our hideous heritage of disharmony and cruelty, disease and pollution had been healed, our planet's karmic state must be holding back that of the greater macrocosm to which we belong. Urgent attention must then be given, by all of us, to such iniquities as vivisection, torture, the destruction of the rain forests, the contamination of land and sea, the abuse of the Third World, the tolerance of aggression and the hypocrisy of arms dealing.

4

The Chakras

Modern physics affirms that everything in our world is formed by energy, and that it is the variations in its vibrational frequencies which make this energy able to manifest in all shades of density, ranging from rocks to gases. Everything then is an integral part of the Whole, constantly exchanging this basic common factor. By becoming aware of this process of exchange, we can employ it far more purposefully. Understanding of the chakras, or energy system of the human body, is a most useful tool to this end.

The concept of chakras is a very old one originating in India and Tibet, but it is now being increasingly recognized in the Western world. The system applies as well to the universe as to the human body.

In a human being the seven principal chakras run from the base of the spine to the crown of the head. Those who are clairvoyant see them as wheels which spin at different speeds according to the state of the person's energy balance and the use being made of each chakra at that particular moment. They can be likened to generators or constellations of energy.

As indicated in the diagram on page 22, the order of the chakras is as follows: root, sacral, solar plexus, heart, throat, brow and crown.

Each of these has a separate identity and function, and when the system is working well, each creates its own special energy. But they are so closely inter-related, that an imbalance in one of them disturbs all the others to a greater or lesser degree; any chakra that

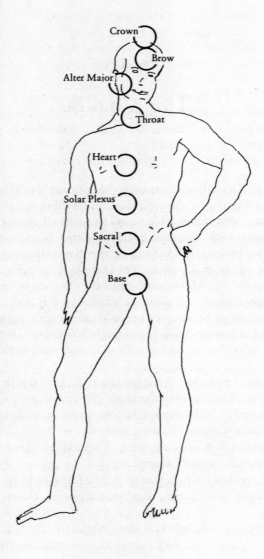

The Human Chakra System

is temporarily depleted can draw off energy from any of the others.

An important element in the good functioning of the team is that the root chakra energy – which can be considered as the person's basic life force – must at all times be feeding the rest of the system with the will to be alive and to be part of the earth. Equally important is the constant flow throughout the body of the divine energy which is accessed through the crown chakra. In the same way that a well-functioning root chakra ensures that a person is able to cope with the practical issues of life, so does the crown chakra ensure that we are in touch with all the spiritual help available to us.

There are many different reasons why a chakra system can be functioning badly. Apart from congenital malformations which may exist in or around one or more of them, there could also be inherited glandular problems (the glandular system corresponds very closely to that of the chakric system). Difficult karma might be another factor working itself out through one or more of the chakras.

In addition to the genetic problems which could be causing chakric imbalance, there are also endless temporary disturbances affecting us, such as stress, emotional upheavals, or fear of any kind.

The difficulties experienced with a chakra usually fall into one of two categories. Either it is over-energized and its frantic quality is disrupting the harmonious working of the team. Or else it has become blocked, and its sluggish movement prevents the person working to full capacity.

The ROOT chakra provides us with our basic 'drive'. It is the chakra most influenced by early traumas, so that if emotional or psychological difficulties occur in childhood, it is here that a very fundamental disequilibrium will assert itself, one which can take many years to rectify. Lack of energy in this chakra immediately induces listlessness, both physically and at other levels. An excess of unused energy here, especially if combined with the over-energization of the solar plexus, can lead to destructive behaviour directed both at oneself and others. The root chakra is also the centre for the sexual energies when they are still at the instinctual level.

The SACRAL chakra deals with all that is regenerative. From here stems all our creativity, which should then be able to express itself through our throat chakra. The concept of creativity is here being used in its widest possible sense, encompassing any thought or action which brings into being something new, from the humblest flower arrangement to the greatest work of art.

It is also in the sacral chakra that the sexual energies move from the instinctual level to a more conscious and complex one. The questions now being dealt with concern an individual's choices about his sexuality. How, for instance, will he deal with the psychological problems arising out of gender roles? How will he express the masculine and feminine principles through himself and his animus/anima?* One of the areas of greatest imbalance in modern mankind, the collective sacral needs much attention and healing. Both excessive sexual activity which brings no satisfaction, and the inability to re-direct this energy into some other creative outlet when sexual expression is unavailable or inappropriate, are causing great pain and difficulties in the world.

The other main concern of this chakra is death and rebirth. By helping us to get in touch with the great natural cycles of constant renewal, it teaches us to flow with our own cycles and to constantly regenerate both ourselves and the world around us. Learning to accept without fear the presence of death in the midst of life is another gift available to us from the sacral.

The SOLAR PLEXUS chakra is the seat of our identity and personal emotions. Any strong feeling, whether it be excitement or anger, fear or love, registers at our midriff: we experience 'butterflies', or feel nauseated. The more unaware and uncontrolled these emotions, the more completely can they take us over, temporarily or long-term. Until we have established our identity and learned to centre ourselves within it, we cannot hope to raise or transform our solar plexus energies to a heart level, where our wiser Self and our emotions can then be used for service to the planet.

Another useful link to be established is one between the solar

* We are all part masculine and part feminine. The anima is the feminine part of a man, and the animus is the masculine part of a woman

plexus and the brow, the former being the home of the intellect, while the latter is connected with mind. If rational thought can be provided by the solar plexus for the expression of that mind, in the same way that the sacral can supply creative energy to the throat, a really strong spiritual self-expression should result.

The solar plexus is the chakra used in psychic work. Those who are developing these abilities should therefore take particular care to keep this centre clear, especially as it is also the chakra most vulnerable to psychic attack. In a situation that could knock you off-centre, whether or not deliberately provoked, place your hands firmly over your ribcage and ask for protection from your guide and helpers.

The HEART chakra marks the divide between what are termed the 'lower' chakras (root, sacral and solar plexus) and the 'higher' ones (throat, brow and crown). The use of the terms 'lower' and 'higher' do not imply any judgment. Neither is inferior nor superior; both are equally important to the well-being of the overall chakric system. So interdependent are they, that the better either group is functioning, the more effectively will the other one work.

In the illustration of the Essene Tree of Life on page 79, one sees very clearly that the more rooted into the earth are the lower chakras, which govern man's relationship with his own personality and the earth, the more can the higher ones soar upwards, allowing full development of his relationship with others and with the heavens.

As the meeting point between the inner and outer, the individual and his world, the heart chakra needs above all to be a point of stillness – this quality being in no way equated with inactivity. Achieving this stillness allows the heart chakra to begin expressing compassion and charity, those qualities which eventually allow us to think and feel beyond ourselves, so that no longer fenced in by our personality, we can take the first steps towards unconditional love. This is a critical initiation point. The future of our planet may well depend on whether enough of us pass through it quickly enough.

As the chakra associated with the higher level of creativity, the

THROAT is closely linked to the sacral centre, from which it can receive immense support if they are in tune. Strongly flowing throat energies engender great satisfaction and fulfillment; if blocked, preventing even the most tentative self-expression, they will cause frustration and eventually illness.

The ALTER MAJOR chakra is not usually included amongst the major chakras, but as it is now beginning to develop actively, it needs recognition so that we can make use of its wonderful gifts. Situated at the base of the skull, it is connected to that instinctual part of our brain which has been almost extinguished by modern life. As the centre of self-preservation, it is what allows the aborigine to locate game and water in a seemingly parched and featureless desert. When still functioning in civilized man, though usually only unconsciously, it is the chakra which saves him from impending danger, compelling him to change carriages just before a train crash in which he would otherwise have been killed.

The alter major is the pre-verbal, pre-emotional chakra. Because of its strong connection with the instincts, it is here that panic or pandemonium attack us. In this sense it is closely related to the energies of the root and solar plexus. For someone to have a well-balanced alter major, a sound relationship between himself and the earth must exist.

The BROW governs the higher mind and the spirit and all that relates to them. Clarity should be its dominant characteristic. Its natural role is as command tower of the other chakras. It mustn't, however, except in the rarest cases, be allowed excessive power. A person ruled by his mind to the exclusion of his heart will fulfill his function on earth no better than someone who allows such excessive rein to his feeling nature that his mind is swamped.

The brow is also the chakra of spiritual vision.

It is through the CROWN chakra that we contact our higher self and those spiritual beings willing to help us. In paintings of Jesus and the saints, this chakra is depicted as a halo.

Certain specific colours have traditionally been associated with each chakra. Starting at the root with red, the colour of the densest vibration, we move upwards to orange for the sacral; yellow for the solar plexus; green for the heart; blue for the throat; reddish brown for the alter major; indigo for the brow, and violet for the crown.

It is perfectly possible to lead a healthy, useful and contented life consciously using only the four lower chakras, the three higher ones remaining relatively unawakened. But once someone has experienced the faintest need or desire for something beyond the material, his thoughts and actions will begin stirring into activity at least one of his higher chakras. A two-way process will then be set in motion: by aspiring towards something greater than himself, that chakra will begin to develop; as it develops, so will his capacity for growth.

5

Healing

The current revival of interest in the art of healing is good news indeed: never before has mankind been in such urgent need. Given the catastrophic mess into which we have sunk, only a force as direct and natural as healing can hope to restore our spiritual bodies to a state of balance and harmony.

The basic principle of healing postulates that an unlimited supply of energy is available from the universe. When we learn to direct that energy where needed, peace and regeneration follow. But before such measures can become really effective in our lives, most of us need to make a major change in attitude towards our health. So discouraged about it have we become that we no longer even expect to feel well. First of all there are all the environmental factors adversely affecting us: bad drinking water, exhaust fumes, food additives, hormone-fed animals, etc. Then most of us are dulled by our jobs which we stagger through, exhausted and anxious, gulping down as 'restoratives' the weekends and holidays which usually do us no good because we are by then too exhausted. Many of us also lead very irregular lives, eating and sleeping without pattern, which leads to dietary problems and insomnia. Modern travel further blackens the picture with unhealthy elements such as jet lag and stress. If we exacerbate these already disastrous living conditions with junk food, cigarettes, drugs and alcohol, we are in real trouble.

Until now we have more or less expected all this to be repaired for us from time to time by the medical services, usually without any active participation from ourselves. But the situation is now too serious. Self-responsibility has become the only hope.

Even if modern urban conditions prevent us from feeling 100% fit, nearly all of us could improve considerably on our present life style. We could, for instance, start paying attention to our body's need for sleep, healthy food, peaceful thoughts and unflustered emotions. In regular meditation (see Chapter 17) we could begin to relax deeply. We could seek help from a therapist or healer. And observing the changes in ourselves, we would be encouraged to continue replacing our state of chronic self-destruction with one of well-being.

Although healing is in a certain sense 'simple' because it uses only energy rather than chemicals or machines, the art of healing is far from simple. Becoming a really good healer requires a lot of study and the on-going commitment to continue working on oneself both psychologically and spiritually. The more pure a channel for the healing energies you can be, the better the results. Anyone wanting to pursue this calling seriously should attend a well-established course, or at least be apprenticed for some time to a competent and experienced healer. This is not a field in which to experiment casually.

Most healing techniques are based on the successful balancing of the energies which are constantly entering the physical body from the surrounding 'subtle' ones. (See diagram on page 30.) Starting with the physical body, which is the densest, the etheric, the astral, the mental and the spiritual bodies vibrate ever faster. It is these subtle bodies which step down to a manageable rate the energies of the spiritual worlds which would otherwise be far too intense for our physical bodies to bear.

When healing is practised, most healers place their hands a few inches away from their patients. This is because it is preferable to work on the etheric body rather than the physical one, as it is in the former that any disease or imbalance already exists before it has manifested physically. The healing power emanating from the practitioner's hands will accomplish two main things: the patient's own self–healing powers will be activated, and energy will start

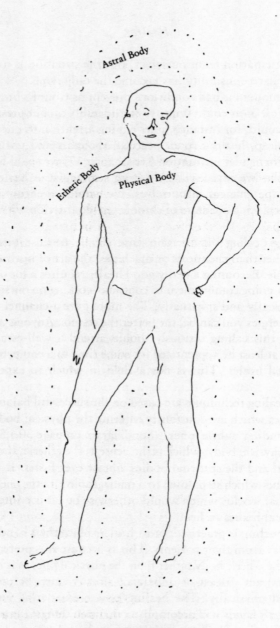

Astral Body

Etheric Body

Physical Body

The Subtle Energy bodies of Man

flowing more harmoniously through his chakras.

It is very important that new patients come to healing in their own time. Although, as with hypnosis, healing cannot be forced on someone against his will, it can be very unnerving to participate in something which one doesn't really understand. Healing a reluctant patient is also unproductive because a barrier will be set up between patient and healer, preventing energy exchange.

The most helpful stance when receiving healing is one of trust and stillness. A patient can also ask that whatever is right should happen. Such an attitude, though seemingly passive, will in fact prove very helpful for the process being set in motion.

Because our free will must be respected by healers as much as by anyone else, it is unacceptable that 'absent' or 'distant' healing (that is to say when the patient is not present), be sent to someone without his consent. There are, of course, exceptions to this rule, such as someone being in a coma; in these cases particular care should be taken to ensure that the healer or healing group do not impose their will and desires onto the patient.

To 'hold someone in the Light', a much more generalized form of healing, is however always all right. One of the most basic laws of healing is that only God knows a patient's true needs. It is therefore imperative always to ask that His will be done. If this request is made with real humility, the healing energies will reach the origins rather than the symptoms of the disease – even if the healer is unaware of them himself.

Under these circumstances the outcome of the healing will also be the right one for the person's overall soul evolution. That may not include an alleviation of his physical suffering, but will almost certainly comprise a shift in his attitude or perspective. This is a difficult premise to accept at first, but it is crucial. A healer is a channel only, and as such it is not up to him to impose anything on the patient.

The reason why 'absent' healing is often as effective as 'contact' healing (and even works better for those healers who find the presence of a patient intimidating), is that neither time nor space exist in the meditative state necessary for giving healing.

Because healing is so in harmony with Aquarian Age ideals, its importance and success will undoubtedly grow, both in the field of health where alternative practitioners are on the brink of many exciting discoveries, and as healers of the earth, working with both ecologists and those who are studying the sacred science of geomancy.

Further exploration of health and disease is made in chapter 19, and discussion of the healer's role in restoring the earth to health takes place in chapter 6.

6

Earth Energies, Ley Lines, Holy Sites, Pilgrimaging

The Earth, like human beings, has energy points which concentrate certain specific types of energy. They are often connected to each other by ley lines, a phenomenon which can be envisaged as psychic channels through which the earth energies flow. In certain places where a number of ley lines meet, there exist power points. These have been recognized as holy sites since the beginning of mankind by all religions concerned with earth power. As the significance of these ley lines emerges for modern man, we may well find them to be of greatest assistance in re-establishing a good working partnership with the Earth.

Esoteric teaching tells us that many aeons ago, great beings came to our planet and laid out this grid as a source of regeneration for both the Earth and its inhabitants. During mankind's very early years, his intuitive sensitivity and his oneness with the Earth were so complete that he never questioned this reality. When choosing sites for worship and astrological research, he naturally placed them where there existed a particularly strong concentration of Earth energies. Some still remain as dolmens and stone circles. The linking of these sites through ley lines further strengthened their psychic power; by being used for the correct purpose, the strength of the ley lines was also confirmed.

It is only since the Age of Reason that cathedrals and churches in the West have no longer been sited according to these norms. Unless built on old sites, they have consequently emanated little power. The Chinese are one of the few people to still honour these beliefs.

Although banned by the Communists in China itself, traditional Chinese all over the world always consult someone trained in the science of geomancy in order to establish a harmonious relationship between the Earth and any new building being erected.

Several drastic factors have been needed in order to re-awaken western man's awareness of these subtle energies flowing through the Earth. The most glaring of these has been the ecological breakdown of the 20th century, dramatically highlighting as it has the need for a changed attitude. Unless we can once again become children of mother earth we cannot receive her strength and nourishment; unless we look after her, she will have no strength to give us.

The second factor is more subtle and results from the scientific discoveries which confirm what the mystics have always asserted: the Earth is not an isolated entity, sufficient unto itself. There is a constant exchange between it and the rest of the Universe. We are as interrelated with the furthest star as with our closest family.

So divorced have we become from this fundamental truth and from our own intuititive nature that it has taken the present day crisis to open our eyes to the changes needed. The natural disasters proliferating throughout the world can leave us in no doubt: the Earth herself must be taken into account rather than 'mastered'. These first glimmers of humility are the first flickers of hope on a very long road.

It was in 1925 that Alfred Watkins published *The Old Straight Track*, the first major book on earth energies. Since then, a few gifted researchers have mapped a large number of ley lines. Two of the major ones are the St Michael line, which runs from the Suffolk Coast at Bury St Edmunds to St Michael's Mount in Cornwall; the other is the St John line running from Nova Scotia to New Mexico. Something which emerges clearly from this study is that each line has specific characteristics and roles to play within the whole. Most of the churches on the St Michael line, for instance, are dedicated to St Michael, a fact which undoubtedly imbues England with that strong inspirational energy connected with this archangel. How different is the warm, feminine, earthy energy generated in South-

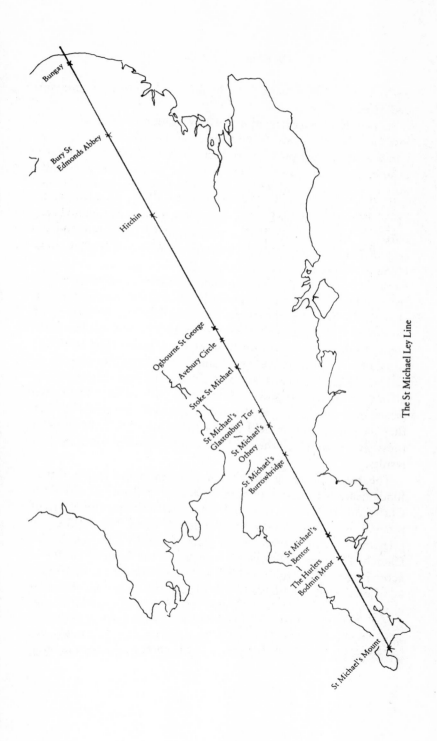

The St Michael Ley Line

Bungay

Bury St
Edmonds Abbey

Hitchin

Ogbourne St George
Avebury Circle
Stoke St Michael
St Michael's
Glastonbury Tor
St Michael's
Othery
St Michael's
Burrowbridge

St Michael's
Bentor
The Hurlers
Bodmin Moor

St. Michael's Mount

ern France and Italy, where the ley lines are defined by churches dedicated to Mary.

As people of exceptional sensitivity gradually re-discover this lost knowledge, the world-wide grid can be mapped, so that we know where power points have been deliberately or inadvertently misused and need healing, where they have been wasted and should now be honoured, and where they are working harmoniously.

Another phenomenon being researched by these pioneers is that of 'corn circles', which are now appearing in increasingly complex patterns. Although little is yet known about them, it is almost certain that they are another response of nature and the cosmic forces to the present conditions on Earth. Through their conformity to the laws of sacred geometry, their persistence, and their recurrence in certain areas, they cannot be considered to arise through chance. The fact that the corn is rarely damaged in the forming of the circles also suggests that they are created by a benevolent force trying to draw our attention to something, rather than being the work of some destructive power simply messing up our fields.

Those engaged in earth energy work usually experience a deeper affinity with certain power points than with others. Their own personality and chakric development combined with past-life work they have done in this field will be the cause of this. Working at those sites with which they feel most in tune will produce the best results.

The form emerging for this new earth pilgrimaging differs fundamentally from that of both the ancient civilizations and of the Christians. It does not seek to drum up earth energies by means of processions and the loud repetitive use of sound. Nor do the new pilgrims limit their reverence to places formally hallowed by the Church. Their sense of service is focussed on the Earth herelf. By re-activating earth energies which have become dormant, they make additional energy available for the planet. If a cathedral, church or chapel already exists on the site they have chosen to work with, they seek to blend its good energies with those newly arising. If there is no building, they recognize and encourage the energies to flow in a balanced and harmonious way. At the end of the 'working', great

Corn Circles on the Salisbury Plain

care is taken to close down the centre formally until further work is undertaken there.

Another matter requiring care is the intention of the pilgrim. Never must he invoke energy in order to gain personal power. This work must be undertaken in a spirit of service. If ego inflation occurs, no good work will be done: there can even be danger to the site and the people involved. These earth forces are very powerful and not to be treated lightly.

If you feel drawn to this work, you can either start on your own or else join a group. If you decide on the former, choose any place to which you feel especially attracted and just sit there quietly, trying to become as aware as possible. Some kind of interaction between yourself and the site will almost certainly happen. When it does, ask, in whatever words seem suitable, for divine energy to enter the surroundings. Do not programme the use to which it is to be put. Simply allow yourself to become the mediator between heaven and Earth, drawing the energy from both of them to meet at this particular point. In this early stage of your exploration, a spirit of love and service is all you will need. Later, as your power to concentrate and direct energy grows, your time spent in this way will become even more fruitful.

Alternatively, you could choose to join a group already engaged in earth energy work. Some of these travel to various sites all over the country, or even abroad, while others confine their activities to a local centre. In group work you will, of course, learn more quickly and be able to do more active work, because once beyond the beginner's stage you will need someone with occult expertise in order to work safely and effectively.

In some teaching, the Earth is said to have chakra points which manifest the same qualities as those found in a human chakric system. At a well-functioning root chakra, for instance, one would expect to find a strong, primary, red-blooded energy. Gdansk in Poland, where Solidarity was born, and Marseille, the heart of the French Mafia, are two good examples of this.

It is at sacral centres that regeneration occurs. Machu Pichu in Peru, where the Inca civilization was born, emits this force.

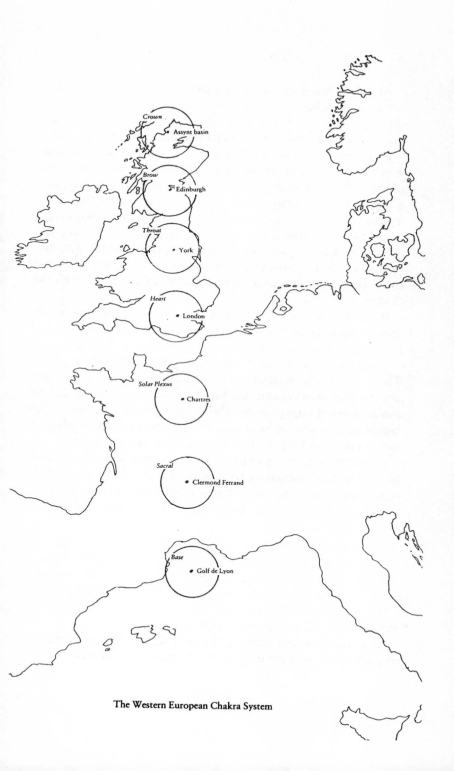

The Western European Chakra System

At solar plexus sites the emotions can be so easily and freely expressed that this is a difficult energy in which to live. Unless one's identity and wiser Self are very clearly defined, places like New York tend to generate muddle and nervous exhaustion.

Heart centres emanate a transpersonal atmosphere from which love and compassion can be easily expressed. Glastonbury, centre of the Arthurian/Avalon legends, is a very good example. But like a person's heart, these places are vulnerable; of all the sites in England, Glastonbury has probably been the most fiercely subjected to psychic attack.

On the throat chakra of Western Europe is found the great cathedral, York Minster. Its beauty, and the music performed there, exemplify the higher forms of creativity associated with that chakra.

Brow chakras attract centres of quiet and learning: universities, great libraries and contemplative orders. Tibetan monasteries high in the Himalayas carry the very essence of a brow chakra's clarity.

From crown chakra sites can be derived much spiritual power. These places, like Krakow in Poland and Reims in France, have always been deemed suitable for the crowning of kings and the consecrating of important members of the Church. Because of their highly rarified atmosphere, they are demanding cities in which to live but are very helpful to those seeking spiritual growth.

As further research is done on power points, ley lines and holy sites, it will be fascinating to have further clarification about the significance and usage of that grid which was laid out – and not completed, some say – by those great Beings of long ago.

7

Guidance

The Piscean Age was the time when spiritual learning came to us as pupils taught by a Master. Obedience and Service were the key words in relationship to those with more learning than ourselves. Now, in the age of the individual, we are being asked to learn in a different way, and this difference will nowhere be more marked than in the field of guidance. Without recourse to others, an ever-increasing number of people will learn to find within themselves that still small voice which can grow increasingly authoritative if we have learned to listen for it with humility, through a channel unencumbered by our own wishes and fears.

Our greatest initial difficulty in establishing contact with something beyond our everyday self will probably lie in trusting a process with which our conscious minds will feel uneasy. Modern education is so bound by left-brain thinking – that is to say the logical masculine approach – that most of us are unfamiliar with the means by which the unconscious tries to communicate. We are not taught, for instance, to listen to dreams and intuitions; in many cases we would be ridiculed for doing so. Rational thought has, of course, a vital role to play, but it must not become so powerful that it excludes from our lives the whole rich world of the unconscious. Unlearning the rigidity inherent in left-brain thinking in order to allow a balance between the rational and the intuitive is therefore the first step. Care must be taken here not to tip too far into right-brain behaviour so that an equally undesirable imbalance is created and one becomes woolly-minded and lacking in discrimination.

The concept of man being divided into lower, middle and higher selves is taught by many spiritual disciplines and some modern schools of psychology, such as psychosynthesis and the transpersonal approaches. Although one can live a perfectly acceptable social and moral life totally unaware of one's Higher Self, once a person has heard the first whispers from that demanding but deeply-rewarding part of himself, whose existence he may not even have suspected, he will have to make a definitive choice between cutting off entirely from these new intimations or re-evaluating his entire life. Once this awareness has been acknowledged, it can be disregarded only with great difficulty and at considerable risk to his well-being.

The initial contact with guidance nearly always comes through the Higher Self. This can occur deliberately, by such spiritual practices as prayer or meditation which promote the tranquility and state of listening in which guidance can gradually be received. It can also happen through the psyche subtly declaring itself available to the voice of the Higher Self. Either way, the first messages often come via the symbolic and apparently topsyturvy world of dreams, whose significance and authority now need to be taken seriously. As we learn to interpret their messages and begin to act upon them, new symbols and indications follow at increasing speed. That mysterious phenomenon of synchronicity begins to produce exactly the right tools for learning at exactly the right speed and in the right order. As the Higher Self is activated, and co-operation grows between the three selves, the relationship between ourselves and the outer world becomes ever richer.

As we have seen, it is through the Higher Self that significant dreams, visions, and purposeful intuitions come. But they are only of practical use if given reality by the lower and middle selves. Anyone who tries to express his life of the spirit – that which gives it meaning and purpose – only through his higher chakras inevitably comes a cropper. We are not given guidance in order to float off with it into a world of illusion and self-inflation. If it is of any value at all, it is there to be firmly grounded into the earth where it can be of use to all of us. This is one of the main messages of the Essene

Tree which cannot be too heavily emphasized.

Once contact with the Higher Self has been firmly established, it is possible to move on to a meeting with one's guide. It is taught esoterically that each of us is given at birth a guide who will remain with us during our whole life unless most exceptional circumstances require a change. It is his role, and great joy, to help us on our spiritual path. Like all members of the Higher Worlds, he is longing to make closer contact with us and will take great strides towards us as soon as we make even a faltering footstep towards him. At the slightest sign of interest or effort on our part we can be certain of receiving immense support, both inwardly and outwardly.

Help from guides other than our own is sometimes given to us, particularly at difficult periods of our lives. Often these turn out to be a discarnate member of our soul group or someone with whom we have worked in similar circumstances during another lifetime. But, as with all guides, whoever they claim to be, intense discrimination must be exercised to make certain that their motives are pure and their judgment sound. This is part of our spiritual training. One of the most dangerous traps is that of absolving ourselves of all responsibility for our guidance, possibly even behaving with monstrous selfishness under the guise of obeying some exalted discarnate teacher. Over and over again, we must question ourselves, making certain that imagination and illusion are not intruding.

If we have two or even three long-term guides, as sometimes happens, common sense and intuition will tell us which one of them to consult at different times. One, for instance, could be more at home with personal issues, another more geared to abstract ideas, and a third particularly adept on all matters relating to the spirit.

Whatever the details of the help available, the important thing is to learn to open the channel through which communication can be received. This is best done with the help of someone experienced in these matters, who can teach you to make the necessary shift in consciousness, and establish that state of expectant receptivity in which preconceived ideas play no part.

Many discarnates (souls at present not in incarnation), long to make contact with the earth, especially if they are closely connected to someone here or to the work they are doing. Those whose motives are pure and who genuinely seek to help us, will leave us absolute free will to accept them into our lives or not. But those who want to manipulate us or further some nefarious work on which they were formerly engaged, will use any means by which to draw attention to themselves and force themselves upon us. It is this fact which makes it so important to exercise stringent discrimination at all times. The cunning of ill-intentioned discarnates is immense and will, with lightning speed, take advantage of any naivety or lack of clarity.

The mechanics of discrimination are not all that easy or straightforward. They require, above all, an active use of the intuition and a willingness to set aside both the fears and longings we may be experiencing about possible communication from discarnates. No genuinely clear impression can be received about the calibre of the discarnate if our own personality is impinging on the picture. Once this detached standpoint has been well established, we should concentrate on recognizing the real nature of what is being offered to us. If we sense the possibility of deception, or even unreliability, it is better to judge wrongly than to trust misguidedly.

Once this first test has been passed, the second phase of discrimination lies in the old adage "By their fruit shall ye know them". Try out their advice without allowing it too much power. Trust only when experience has conclusively taught you that it is justified. Remember always that we are under no obligation to enter into the dialogue offered. We can opt out at any moment for any reason. We can also go forward at exactly the speed we choose. If it is laziness which governs our decision to disregard guidance, we will probably have to face the issue again at some future date, but that too is our own decision.

When considering a discarnate's state of development and its qualifications for helping us, two things should be remembered. The first is that passing through 'death' into a different state of consciousness accords one no special knowledge or wisdom. The range of spiritual development amongst discarnates must therefore be as great as that amongst incarnates. We would not blindly accept advice from any old living person; the same must apply to our relationship with the 'dead'. The second fact to remember is that the spiritual law of attraction operates as effectively in the Higher Worlds as it does on earth. All souls who 'pass over' gravitate to the exact level where they belong from an evolutionary point of view. It is to this fact that Jesus referred when He said, "In my Father's house there are many mansions". So between earth lives the discarnate in question will be in the company of those whose level of understanding is the same as his. When challenging an entity who is proffering guidance, we must ascertain the level from which it is coming. This needs to be done with humility, but also with clarity. There is no value in receiving knowledge which is beyond the range of our understanding; nor should we settle for banal communications that teach us nothing.

Anyone who decides to live in accordance with the mysterious language of guidance, whether from his Higher Self or from a discarnate, will almost certainly experience many difficulties in his life, especially as the guidance becomes more exacting. But he will in recompense find himself given wonderful opportunities to improve the quality of his spiritual life. This will happen not only through his own guidance, but also through the group connections spoken of in other chapters. Because of the intricate linking between group members and ever-higher levels, he will now be able to call on help from those members of his group presently discarnate, and also from any source of guidance available to other group members. This multiplicity and diversity of assistance carries only one obligation: that the best use be made of anything received.

8
Ecology

During the Sixties, the word ecology carried slightly cranky, fringe connotations. When brown leather sandals and long hair were the hallmark of the people first drawing our attention to the Earth's desperate plight, it was easy for society to take them lightly. But when the Seventies produced 'Green' political parties in several countries, the movement began taking on weight. As the sandals and Indian clothes were replaced by tidy sweaters, the mocking voices grew sparser. The establishment of the World Wildlife Fund, Friends of the Earth and Greenpeace heralded a great outbreak of concern for our imperilled fauna and flora. The instigators and supporters of ecology now included people with considerable knowledge of economics, biology and botany. The first-rate nature programmes produced for television made a wide-spread impact. So did the statistics which made it impossible to ignore the fact that the world could easily be rendered utterly chaotic if the wealthy countries' only concern was for their further enrichment.

During the Eighties, a wide section of the public came to realize that ecology is not about the survival of an obscure species of white rhino; it is the survival of mankind and our planet which is at stake. The destruction of the rain forests and the resulting climatic changes will increase global warming and the level of carbon dioxide. If nothing is done to prevent further damage to the ozone layer, ultra-violet radiation will increase, and so will the incidence of skin cancer. Global warming will cause the ice caps to melt and the consequent flooding will be disastrous. These predictions are not the speculations of doom-mongers; they are well-documented facts researched by some of the world's most eminent scientists who, in increasing numbers, are joining the ranks of the ecologists. No one can any longer pretend that the dangers do not exist.

This new awareness has already produced some positive effects. These happenings are now being brought to the world's attention with far more frequency and punch. No longer can the desecrators suppress publicity about the devastation being perpetrated. Nor can their activities any longer be silently condoned by the world in the name of progress. The public is beginning to demand facts, and there are more and more people willing to give them.

Those strong factions all over the world still resisting the ecological call are motivated by either the immediate desire to survive or else by financial greed. In South America, for instance, many of the most caring people are of necessity so concerned about their children dying of malnutrition that the whole question of the Amazon jungle becomes of secondary importance. At the other end of the spectrum are most of the world financiers, whose total dedication to profit is so great that no other considerations are allowed to interfere. Little change can be expected from this powerful group until considerable pressure is exerted on them, or their methods become self-defeating.

Already the fury of the Third World is gaining power and voice against the Northern capitalists, who strip their countries' assets and foment crime and unrest while purporting to bring employment and opportunity. Even some of those governments which have in the past aided and abetted their country's destruction for the sake of temporary prosperity and additional tax money, are now beginning to demand new solutions.

It is becoming evident that the world's resources, which have taken millions of years to form, cannot be left to the mercy of business; too many times has it proven itself entirely lacking in any form of morality. The Earth's often irreplaceable resources are not the prerogative of the rich, but the resonsibility of the world's entire population. From this fact is slowly emerging the glimmering of a new business/social morality. The initiative of business itself, 'green investment funds' are becoming increasingly popular; only companies that do not pollute the environment or act in a manner contrary to its interests are elegible for investment by these funds.

Human apathy has probably been the greatest danger faced by our planet during this wild binge of exploitation. So accustomed did we become to our warrior-like attitude towards our home that our reaction, if we noticed anything at all, was one of despondency. How could we hope to reverse such a gigantically complex process? we asked ourselves miserably, and did nothing. Now, thank goodness, as we stand on the edge of the precipice, the desire and the will to fight for our planet's life seems to be implanting itself in many individuals and groups. More and more options are being given to us to do something constructive, however small. Even if only dimly, most people now know that something has gone badly wrong and must be put right. A sense of urgency is gradually spreading. Ecology in the Nineties is not only respectable, but vitally necessary.

With the rise into the collective consciousness of these new realizations, ideas which seemed to be an inalienable part of our thinking are starting to crack up. Leaving aside the immorality of the issue, a high 'standard of living' for a small portion of the world cannot, for instance, be seen as a sensible target if it brings about the 'greenhouse effect', which in turn will result in climatic change, drought, desertification and famine. Amazing scientific progress cannot be justified if its side-effects include such intense pollution of the land and oceans that we can no longer consume their fruits.

People's new sense of world citizenship is also working indirectly to spread ecological principles. However passionately national identity is being sought politically by many minorities, it is becoming obvious that if disaster is to be averted, world resources must eventually be globally protected. Countries like Ethiopia, for instance, must be helped to break the patterns which encourage desertification. Allowing their tribes systematically to wear out the land and then move on to do the same elsewhere is bringing famine and disease not only to their own land and people, but it is also disrupting the entire planet's climate. Non-renewable resources

such as coal and oil can no longer be exploited for profit. The abo-
lition of pollution will also soon have to become a matter for world
legislation. Small scale projects which encourage people not to
waste or destroy can start reversing the present situation, at the
same time that the problem is tackled on an international scale.

The number of people needed to bring about a new awareness is
in fact very small. It was through the efforts of a tiny minority that
slavery and child labour became unacceptable. Now it is the
recognition of our interrelatedness with all things which will bring
about our next step forward. That accomplished, we will never
again see ourselves as ants perched on the surface of a dead entity
towards which we have no responsibility.

From a spiritual viewpoint, the main fact about ecology which
glares at us is man's long-standing disregard for the symbiotic
relationship he was intended to have with the Earth, each depending on and providing for the other. When we began to see ourselves
as masters of the earth rather than its stewards, this relationship
was destroyed. We have effectively forgotten that it is our duty to
maintain a state of balance in the Earth's resources.

The violent and excessive mining methods we have used, our
depletion of the soil and massacre of our woodlands have made
inevitable that we lose that security and joy the Earth offered us.
Until we know that we and the Earth form part of a physical and
mystical whole, both infinitely precious, the chaos and strife on
Earth can only worsen.

Christian teaching has always assured us that because of this
unity, not the smallest sparrow can fall without all else being
modified. Events in the Sahara affect everyone everywhere. The
decisions taken in the offices of the World Bank ripple out over all
our lives. On the same principle, everything within the Universe is
also inter-connected. No star or planet remains unaltered by events
here. What happens to us ecologically is then quite literally of
cosmic importance. To avoid what is unsound is no longer enough;
we must work urgently for positive ecological health.

Logically there is no hope of achieving this, so far have we
plunged towards self-destruction. Yet, because we are part of a

greater whole which needs us as much as we need it, help in saving our planet will be given to us if we can just make that leap beyond totally materialistic thinking.

9

Suffering and Loss

The American Constitution asserts that 'the pursuit of happiness' is one of man's basic goals. Robert Louis Stevenson also speaks most positively about happiness: "There is no duty we so much underrate as the duty of being happy", he affirms. In both cases the assumption is made that it is possible for man to be in a fundamentally satisfactory relationship with himself, the world and God. Because the term 'happiness' has become so debased that it now carries an ephemeral, almost frivolous overtone, let us replace it for the moment with the word joy and consider whether it is a quality or state of being for which we can – or should – diligently seek.

Although not a right, something which can be bestowed upon us from outside, joyfulness is a God-given natural state. That most of us have been alienated from it through thousands of years of conflict with our true selves does not change this fact. By steadily re-aligning ourselves with our soul's purpose, we can connect again on a deep and permanent level with that state of joy; once established, it can remain actively alive whatever the assaults made on it by suffering and loss.

The muddled thinking which has led us to believe that happiness is a right rather than a goal has engendered an equally erroneous idea that all suffering and loss are totally negative events, to be avoided at all cost wherever possible. The juxtaposition of these two attitudes inevitably creates much disgruntlement, we think we should have things we haven't got and we resent much of what we have.

This assumption that happiness is due to us has also helped produce a vast number of neurotics in constant search of something they cannot define – let alone attain. Inextricably entwined with such a search is a terror of suffering, so stultifying that it blocks the way for any change which might ultimately bring them joy. Having equated change with loss and loss with suffering, they will prefer to stay trapped in their own misery rather than risk altering anything. This disastrous pattern has become so engrained in our society that we hardly question how ill-equipped most of us are to face suffering, or even new situations. We consider it quite natural that people do everything in their power not to be confronted with pain, forgetting that much valuable learning can be wasted through such defendedness.

An excessive allocation of suffering is another matter and can prove very unconstructive. Depression or some form of addiction can easily result. Alternatively the person may end up encased in an impenetrable shell, or else be so emotionally flayed that it will take him many years, perhaps even several lifetimes, to recover.

But, mercifully, such cases are rare. Spiritual law promises us that we will be given only that for which we have the strength. Being overwhelmed by sorrow implies then either that total despair is a rare but necessary part of a person's karma, or, that he is stronger than he realized and that by putting himself into this crisis situation he may well have provided himself with the best possible setting for accessing new strength and guidance. In Chinese calligraphy the character for crisis is very encouraging, containing within itself the symbols for both danger and opportunity.

In most cases, once the crisis period is over, the suffering can be appreciated as having been an invaluable tool for growth and self-knowledge as well as a means for clearing karma. It can also often teach deep compassion and the ability to help others. Few people's heart chakras are truly open until they have experienced considerable pain.

Knowing that we ourselves choose the basic circumstances of our lives does help make painful events easier to accept. If our life has a pattern and meaning which we recognized between earth lives, and if our suffering is part of that pattern, it too has meaning, and is therefore bearable. If there is intelligent guidance permeating the universe at all levels, our pain is surely not wasted: it can be transmuted into a redemptive force. Anger and resentment can become redundant if we choose to understand and use what has happened to us instead of hastily bundling it all under the carpet. The experience of surviving the pain can also help free us from much fear.

Trying to make life smooth and innocuous for ourselves or others is a form of insult, implying that we have no guts. It is also injurious to the development of our courage and powers of endurance. Unfortunately much modern medicine and psychotherapy encourages this sort of non-confronting. Sleeping pills and tranquilizers by the bushel are doled out to prevent the doctor or the patient facing the cause of the problem. Psychotherapists also frequently perform psychic cosmetic jobs, which simply smooth over the effects of trauma with a view to re-integrating the patient into society as speedily as possible. Wallowing in our pain is a waste of time, but accepting it and working through it with courage can be very rewarding.

Whether we like it or not, life consists of change. If we resist this fact, we live in a constant state of regret for all that has passed and altered. If we accept it, we can live each day in the Now, and the changes can be seen as a series of initiations taking us always forwards. When we are going with the stream of our own and greater cycles instead of fighting them, we will experience a minimum sense of loss within the changes.

In olden times all initiations were ritualized; the prospective candidate was told by the priest or priestess when he was ready for the next stage. Now, to the fullest extent to which each of us is capable, we are called upon to produce our own curriculum of psychological and spiritual growth. And we must determine our own speed of progress. It is often here that we cause ourselves that spiritual pain which is almost the hardest of all to bear. Should we move forward frantically fast, we risk overstepping ourselves, and the resulting arrogance and self-aggrandizement will breed their own pain. Should we move ridiculously slowly, showing neither determination nor courage, the pain of non-fulfillment makes our lives desolate. This is part of the spiritual adulthood promised to us for the Aquarian Age.

For anyone whose suffering is holding him in a vice, the help of an enlightened therapist can be invaluable. Guided imagery, dream work, Gestalt, or whatever seems appropriate, can release one from the most long-standing pain. Difficult as it is to transmute suffering into joy, it can be done. And it is worth any effort. For in the same way that every grain of wisdom and every positive action swells the healing potential of the collective unconscious, so too does every joy.

10

Forgiveness

Forgiveness is a key issue in all New Age thinking. Clearing from the totality of our past those situations where anger and resentment still bind us because we have not forgiven or been forgiven, is certain to release much energy. That our efforts will be well worthwhile is certain: as in all psychological and spiritual work, what is done on a personal level reflects into the collective. With the freeing of each knot caused by an unforgiven situation, we reduce not only our own burden of hatred and guilt, but also that of mankind.

Until very recently, the granting of the forgiveness we required for ourselves fell almost entirely under the aegis of the Church, which could bestow or withhold pardon for our sins according to an inflexible set of rules. Not allowed to approach God directly, we needed the intercession of the Church's saints; our prayers complete, we needed a priest to tell us the conditions under which we would be forgiven. Only when this ritual had been observed and our slates wiped clean for us, could we enjoy a comfortable conscience and feel happy at having been re-instated in a loving relationship with our maker.

Although this system treated us as children and deliberately prevented us growing up, it did have one great advantage: it spared us the heavy accumulations of guilt which so bedevil our present world. But it is not a way suited to the Aquarian Age and is gradually losing its power. We can no longer expect to have forgiveness bestowed upon us by an institution mediating between us and God. Taking responsibility for our own lives includes being directly responsible to ourselves and to God for our actions.

Another aspect of the old system which is no longer appropriate for today, was the fact that a supplicant could quite easily remain on a superficial level with regard to the wrong for which he was requesting absolution. He did not have to delve too deeply into his psyche; his sin could be exteriorized by being handed to the priest. Now any admission of guilt must be fully integrated into the psyche; so must its forgiveness. Otherwise the event is merely automatic rather than potentially soul-changing.

Our need for forgiveness is as great, if not greater, than ever before. This becomes painfully obvious whenever people talk about their lives, regretting a divorce or a broken friendship, or a conflict over some material question. Under the old system, if you had wronged someone, part of the penance imposed by the priest consisted of asking that person's forgiveness. Again this is no longer appropriate. Only a forgiveness arising out of real compassion and the desire to transcend past events has the power conclusively to dispel the results of our wrong action. Recognizing instinctively that a significant soul-dredging rarely took place under the old Church system, we often think of forgiveness as a wishy-washy way out. This has made us underrate the potential of true forgiveness, which by letting go and moving on empowers all concerned.

The patently absurd image of Jesus as 'meek and mild' has been another factor which for centuries falsified the truth that forgiveness is not only essential, but also one of the most difficult and painful things to achieve. Even He experienced great anguish and reluctance before being able to love all His neighbours as Himself.

In those schools of psychology most in tune with the New Age, such as psychosynthesis and transpersonal psychology, this need for forgiveness plays a central role – especially the need to forgive oneself. Carrying around a hopeless burden of things we have or haven't done serves no useful purpose; it only prevents us from recognizing our own capabilities and path.

Childhood, that time when we were most vulnerable and have often been most harmed, is a major area in which to embark on forgiveness. If we have for years (either buried or consciously seething within ourselves) harboured a whole constellation of hatreds and resentment from our youth, we will never be happy or fulfilled until we have made a strong, selfmotivated act of forgiveness towards those who perpetrated the pain. Only then can it disperse, its energy freed for something creative. To forgive truly is to disempower the person or situation that has been draining us. The whole past can be changed in this way. That part of us which was once static and useless can be re-integrated into a new, richer whole. We can begin to live in the Now.

Out of those personal acts of forgiveness can grow collective ones. And for these to take place is of paramount importance, for the world is pockmarked with sites where dreadful things have happened, and where hatred and bitterness now constellate in a most destructive way. If those who have been in concentration camps, or been exiled, or imprisoned and tortured, can begin to forgive, however tentatively, their gaolers and torturers, light will start to enter these dark patches in our globe. A most valuable and rewarding work for either individuals or groups lies in reinforcing these people's efforts through prayer and meditation.

The old 'Eye for an Eye and a Tooth for a Tooth' morality must come to an end. Retribution and the thirst for revenge must no longer spread their strangulating tentacles across the Earth. Hatred is a very dangerous emotion, linking us to the object of our hatred as fiercely as does love. None of us wants to be receiving the psychic vibrations of a depraved Buchenwald surgeon or a mad Idi Amin, or of anyone who has harmed us personally. Yet it is our hatred which keeps those vibrations pulsating with life. It is only through unconditional forgiveness, personal and collective, that their power can be broken.

Forgiveness of the dead is another subject to which transpersonal psychologists are giving much attention, for it is often the deceased who are barring our progress. Contrary to what we have long been taught, death does not deprive us of the opportunity to either forgive or be forgiven. Through the 'visualisations' now being used by many therapists, a client is able to see in his imagination the people or situations needing attention. It is often the forgiveness of or from a deceased parent or friend which is the key to this work. Through the combining of the therapist's skills with the amazing wisdom of the client's subconscious, which infallibly knows what pictures it must produce in order to achieve a difficult resolution, many such releases are taking place. If, for instance, forgiveness is being sought for or from someone who has always been a symbol of terror, he or she may well appear in the visualisation in a very vulnerable situation: as a child perhaps or very ill. Compassion can then overcome terror, and forgiveness becomes easier. These techniques can, of course, be equally effective in any interaction between two people who are still alive.

To forgive or to be forgiven is not easy. The journey towards it often includes reliving very painful episodes and letting down the drawbridge into one's most defended inner fortress. But it is always worth the effort.

11

Death

In the same way that life consists of a series of initiations, so is it also a series of small deaths. As we pass through the stages of babyhood, adolescence, adulthood, middle and old age, the previous one dies. The termination of our present incarnation can then be seen as the continuation of an ordered pattern, more intense than the smaller deaths, but neither different in quality nor more final. We have experienced innumerable deaths in the past and will do so again in the future.

In addition to these age-related cycles which we could almost consider as practice runs for dying, we also experience throughout our lifetime the minor deaths occasioned by those separations from a person or place which require that we die to some part of our selves. The more thoroughly these minor deaths can be understood and accepted as part of the human condition, the more calmly and successfully will the eventual death of the physical body take place.

Distressingly few people in the modern western world take advantage of these opportunities for gradually becoming familiar with death. Instead they expend a great deal of energy locking it into a cupboard, refusing even to look at it until it stares them in the face. This is a waste of the help we are constantly being offered. Familiarity dispels fear. To die in fear is the most wasteful thing of all.

The actual circumstances of our dying can be painful or shocking, but death itself is neither a stranger nor frightening. It is no more than a change of consciousness for which we can be ready at all times, travelling lightly so that our load can be laid down whenever we are asked to. The fear of death as a black hole of nothingness, which so haunts many people, is forever dispelled when we accept the reality of former lives. The state of death then becomes a temporary one, a period of rest and re-assessment.

From many accounts given by people who have died clinically and been resuscitated (an occurrence known as the 'near-death-experience'), the actual transition into death is far from unpleasant, whatever the pain endured beforehand. Drawn through a tunnel, at the end of which stands a beautiful being of Light, the dying person knows himself safe and loved. If, as is obviously the case of all 'near-deathers', it is not yet time for him to die and he returns to Earth (a voluntary decision nearly always taken because he realizes that his life's work is not yet completed), this decision nearly always occasions a sense of heavy effort and sacrifice rather than being experienced as a joyful relief. What more convincing proof could we have that beauty, peace and contentment await us 'on the other side'? At a time when the fear of death lies like a black fog over our world, these people return to Earth almost like messengers from God, reassuring us that our fears can be safely discarded, and encouraging us to die our death with love and dignity.

Many sensitives and mediums are also now receiving new information from discarnate sources concerning the nature of life immediately after death, and the various stages through which we pass before again incarnating. It seems from all accounts that after being welcomed by those whom we have most loved on Earth, and being allowed a period of rest, we are shown in full detail our recent life. No judgment is made in the earthly sense; we simply know with total clarity all our lifetimes' thoughts and actions, failures and successes. It is in reconciling ourselves to this life-review – which can be devastating because no self-deceptions will be allowed to protect us from the truth – that we need the unstinting help and love of our guides and teachers. One of their main tasks is to help us assess this life in relation to our total evolution. From this inter-change will gradually emerge the ingredients of our next life on Earth. How long it will be before we have fully assimilated the significance and consequences of our recent life and are ready to take on new experiences, depends partly on the stage of our spiritual evolution and partly on the intensity of the life we have just experienced. On the former also depends the extent to which we can participate in the planning of our next incarnation. Nothing will ever be imposed upon us, but more guidance will be needed if we have not yet reached that stage from where we can view our overall life cycle with objectivity.

The workings of this interim period are highly complex, depending as they do on many factors, such as the relationship between a soul and his group. Here again, more information is gradually being received from the higher worlds so that understanding of these intricate patterns can emerge. In the meantime, it is certain that while between earth lives we are constantly learning, and that we are in the company of those to whom we are most closely spiritually linked. The law of attraction operates with the same certainty in the after life as it does on earth. There where our soul's deepest needs can be met will we find ourselves.

Introduction to Part Two

If the ideas discussed in the foregoing chapters are accepted – or at least taken on board for a trial run – our attitude towards almost everything will alter fundamentally. In the second half of this book I would like to discuss some of these new attitudes and how they could affect our lives.

12

Family and Childhood

For many years it has been fashionable – and delightfully convenient – to fob off onto the older generation all responsibility for our problems, our neuroses and our faults. Either they were so strict that they inhibited us, or else they were so lenient that self-discipline was never learned. Either their expectations were so high that we gave up in despair, or else they didn't care and we have lacked self-esteem ever since. The poor parents, or their substitutes, could not win. Whether they were alcoholics or teetotalers, zealots or atheists, clucking mother-hens or Doctor Spockers, they were certain to have got it wrong.

But since self-responsbility is such a basic ingredient of New Age thinking, this disastrous attitude must be made obsolete immediately: if you have difficulty with the idea that we actually choose the family situation which would be the most appropriate for the lessons we are to learn this time – try for the moment to keep an open mind on it. If it is true we must begin by recognizing all that was positive and helpful in it instead of wallowing in its negative aspects. What were we meant to learn from it? In what way has it prepared us for our work? What particular skills and strengths has it elicited from us – often by the very nature of its problems? And also – what did we fail to learn which still needs exploring?

If life is a training ground, our early years must be the ideal time at which to work on those aspects of our character most needing attention. Difficulties existing between us and those with whom we had to live as children often stem from past life connections. And it is in these very intense and vulnerable years that the debts of the past can best and most quickly be redeemed. Conversely, people we have loved in the past are often close family members who can equally help us – though by gentler means. When viewed as part of the resolution of difficult karma, even the most deprived or cruelty-ridden childhood can be seen as the best setting in which to redress past imbalances or open a previously closed heart. The child can, of course, also have chosen to be the teacher rather than the pupil in any particular situation.

In the same way that childhood often provides the circumstances through which the most intense karmic situations can be resolved, so can it be the time when the deepest karmic debts are incurred for the future. The power struggles and temper tantrums, the anger, greed and envy often brought up by family interaction can enmesh one with other people for many lifetimes.

In the improved relationship between generations which will gradually emerge, possessiveness will have no part. Parents will have realised that nothing is more disastrous than to rob children or adolescents of their power to make choices and decisions. As man's creative capacity increases, this will become even more important. Although parents have a strong duty to build a favourable environment for their children's growth, they do not in any way own them; although their ideas and standards can be taught by example, they cannot be imposed. Once clear guidelines for the child's physical, psychological and spiritual safety and behaviour have been laid down, his free will is as sacrosanct as that of his parents. Neither emotionally nor economically may he ever be blackmailed in an effort to make him conform. This could in some cases even constitute a disastrous curtailment of the evolution of the child, who could quite possibly be more advanced than its parents, especially now when so many evolved souls are incarnating.

13

Education

The true role of education is to draw out a person, to develop his powers of thought and to encourage the gift of intellectual curiosity. Sadly, most modern educators treat their pupils as mini-computers into which facts are stuffed, whether or not they are of any interest or relevance to the children. Jammed into a school 'stream' according to a very questionable method of selection, they are then simply conditioned to fulfill a certain function in society. This attitude towards learning has, generally speaking, produced a race of students so occupied with storing exam data that no time is left for creative study.

Because of constantly changing teachers, the impersonality of huge schools and the ever-increasing mobility of the students themselves, the assessments made of a child's ability are often faulty, or at best inadequate. Without detailed knowledge of his personality and home conditions, sadly the selection board often either wastes children's abilities or else pushes them beyond their natural capacity. Both groups suffer.

Mankind is now going through a radical evolutionary jump, which will involve an enormous change in consciousness. The whole field of education is bound to be affected. Once we have realized that most of the children we are teaching are already familiar with earthlife, it will become obvious that we can no longer simply classify them by age, intelligence, achievement etc. Each student will become an individual, assessed on his potential, but also on his ability to make conscious the skills and knowledge learned in former lives. This will, of course, necessitate the training of teachers who can 'see' into the child's past and then teach him to give it a voice. So much of what we once knew is very close to the surface; with skilful handling, it can become part of our present life.

In order to avoid boredom and/or rebellion at a very profound level, outwardly similar children who are at vastly disparate stages in their spiritual journey will be treated quite differently. For those who already 'know' many things from past lifetimes, remembering them will be the most important part of their education. Onto this base can be added further knowledge and modern skills. For those who are still young to earthlife, more fundamental teaching will be given.

Our present assumption that schoolteachers are automatically equipped by their training to teach the young will for the same reasons be seen as a fallacy. Under our present system, someone could well be 'teaching' a child far more advanced than himself. Ultimately, children will take up their education where it left off in a previous incarnation; teachers and pupils will be matched at a soul level, to the benefit of both parties.

Another major shift in the field of education will result from the contents of the collective unconscious becoming more accessible to an increasing number of people. Within this vast storehouse of knowledge is said to be recorded all the events and thoughts that have ever occurred. Safely stored as part of mankind's heritage, this unimaginable treasure has until now been available only to those with highly-developed psychic powers, or to the geniuses of one field or another who have tapped it in an inspirational rather than a conscious way. Now it seems possible that we will learn to draw directly from it, a study we will start at a young age.

The more incarnations we have already experienced, especially those where learning was a prominent feature, the more easily is knowledge, both old and new, available to us, our learning patterns being already well developed. As these are encouraged in children, the stuffed-computer syndrome will disappear; our greatest asset will become the ability to create a state of mind into which knowledge can be drawn.

This exciting development confirms many communications from Higher Worlds imploring us to realize that our potential is truly unlimited. Not only have we access to the planet's entire past, we can also learn through inner guidance from the whole spiritual hierarchy. Until now this has been difficult for us to believe, so conditioned were we to thinking of ourselves as negligible and temporary inhabitants of Earth. But gradually it is becoming clearer that this promise is not an idle one and that we must start making practical use of the possibilities available to us. In the New Age, unlimited growth will be the goal of children and adults alike. Education – the drawing out of our potential – will become a fascinating, on-going part of our lives instead of a boring preparation for an uninteresting task.

14

Jobs and Careers

In the Western world, where material success has long been the touchstone, the achiever has been the one of whom his parents were proud. If his school career produced good marks, membership of several school teams and a bevy of friends, they felt satisfied and looked forward to him either passing tidily into university, or else moving smoothly into a safe and recognizable job. With any luck, marriage to an equally suitable partner would follow at the appropriate time. The obediently smiling faces in the family photograph album would prove beyond doubt that all was well in the best of worlds.

Against such a background has the Piscean westerner pursued his career for the past century. Although ostensibly behaving in complete freedom, he was, with few exceptions, in reality hideously trapped. Even the token rebellion of his youth was part of the pattern graciously condoned by family and society as long as it lasted for only a reasonable period. From it he emerged unscathed, any deviant ambitions and frustrations sacrificed to the family album, whose record of his life would propitiate a far more profound need in him than any display of individuality. So deeply engrained was this desire to conform and prove himself, that he seldom acknowledged, or even recognized, his life as a voluntarily-accepted prison. If slight qualms ever fingered him, they were quickly shaken off, not only because too many other people's lives were by now inextricably entwined with this success-oriented structure, but also because he would be a nothing without it – both in his own eyes and those of the world.

This obsession with achievement is already slackening and will ultimately die. Success will be quantified by what we are as much as by what we do. Our lives will also be assessed from a much broader viewpoint: what we have accomplished ourselves will be seen as only part of our life's work; what we initiate for others to carry further will be considered of equal importance. When our present working life is seen as a very small part of our total development over the centuries, a failure to reach 'The Top' or the untimely truncating of a career will no longer feel like a total disaster as it does now. It will be the care and creativity we contributed to the job that will matter.

In the present difficult transition period between these two modes of behaviour, it is not surprising that great anguish and alarm are being felt by those parents whose children are beginning to behave in an Aquarian way. They are rejecting the set, life-long job and seeking more flexibility and self-expression. They are demanding more time for exploration before committing themselves. But because they have failed so far to fully grasp the stringent requirements for self-responsibility set by the new impulse, they are in most cases acting out only part of it. Until they pick up the entire new work ethic, adjectives such as shiftless, ambitionless, undisciplined and sponging will continue to be used in describing a behaviour which is so alien to the older generation and so deeply threatens their own self-image.

For a few more years, undeterred, the young will drift or travel, taking temporary jobs, always refusing to declare for a job or career until long after the statutory date set by society. If they eventually join the 'rat race', it will be a voluntary decision rather than the inevitable outcome of their parents' expectations. As the cut-throat world against which they are protesting, at whatever level, gradually crumbles, it will be possible for the young of future generations to express the totality of the new impulse.

During this interim period, because the issues at stake are so fundamental, deep quarrels and rifts, especially between fathers and sons, will inevitably occur. Breakdowns in any system always cause personal conflict. But whether we like it or not, that old system is going, and it is those who can respond to the powerful forces instigating these changes who are the agents of a great shift in behaviour patterns which is vital to our next move forwards. Even our present widespread unemployment, far from being a total disaster, is a major positive factor in bringing about this shift.

It is the change in consciousness of a whole generation that is in question, and we passionately need the many evolved souls amongst them to be as amply equipped as possible. For many young people today, it is the experience of living and being and searching which actually constitutes their career. And however hard this is for the older generation to accept, they must try to do so, because otherwise they will be laying on the young a load of disapproval and guilt very detrimental to the freedom of their search. For many of them it may well take two thirds of their lives to garner from their soul's wisdom all that is needed in order for them eventually to make their contribution to the world. Their's is a multi-disciplined, strenuous and time-consuming treasure hunt which cannot be hurried.

It does not, however, constitute an excuse for 'copping out' and not earning one's daily bread. A basic Aquarian principle states that we should work to provide our needs, not our wants. Earning enough to live reasonably is part of this training, helping also to liberate the individual, and ultimately society, from the frantic message of the advertising firms which have been so deeply engrained into us. Possessions do not equal happiness. There is no reason on earth why we should have to keep-up-with-the-Joneses.

Specialization as practised in the Piscean Age is another concept which will gradually be released. People will try not to develop certain talents and aspects of themselves to the detriment, even annihilation, of the whole. Specialized knowledge will always be necessary, but the vision of the entirety must not be lost. In the same way, people will consciously attempt to act always as a complete person. Scientists, for instance, will no longer so concentrate their work through the brow chakra that their hearts remain unused; nor will artists consecrate themselves so exclusively to the expression of their throat chakras that their practical life becomes chaotic.

In the wonderful expansion of consciousness which is about to take place, and which will allow us to encompass far more within one lifetime than we have been able to until now, the younger generation must not be encumbered, either through fear or lack of imagination, by the limitations of the past. For those who are not on the particular quest of which we have spoken, their choice of job or career will still be very important for their self-fulfillment, but it will not be the determining factor in the 'success' or 'failure' of their life. When we are no longer trying to jam our entire earth experience into three score years and ten, we will have a very different attitude towards time. The one-pointed, bull-dozing desire for 'success' will phase itself out. The search for our inner authority will become the central theme and raison d'être of our life.

15

Authority

In the past forty years, people's attitude towards authority has changed dramatically. Before World War II, nearly everyone had inculcated in them a respect for all those who to some degree or other wielded power. Starting with our parents and continuing into school life, this deference gradually extended to more public authority, including the police, the military, the civil service and the government. Even those who disagreed with the latter's politics paid respect to its representatives, generally assuming that those in power possessed attributes and training which qualified them to govern. Except for declared revolutionaries or members of a persecuted minority, patriotism was another accepted premise which bolstered the general feeling that Authority, including the Church, was working on our behalf.

The war years blew all this apart. Ever since then we have witnessed an escalating revolt against authority in all spheres. When young Americans refused to fight in Vietnam, they upturned the most time-honoured traditions. Protest marches and peace camps, used in a wide variety of circumstances, are now an intrinsic feature of modern life. Even terrorism and violence have become a familiar means by which to gain one's ends. Generally speaking, the voice of the Church is no longer heeded by either individuals or governments – a situation previously unthinkable. Not surprisingly, with such disastrous models all around them, modern children have become increasingly difficult for their parents and teachers to handle, many of them now even viewing the police and other authority figures as the enemy.

A total collapse of the hierarchies we once knew seems imminent.

Economic and political stability appear to have flown irrevocably out of the window.

All over the globe security is being shattered by fighting or by the results of drug-trafficking.

Even nature, our natural ally, is mirroring our disarray; volcanoes and earthquakes and climatic changes are striking at our fondest dreams of a technologically tamed world.

At first sight, in our understandable fear, all this appears to be a total disaster. But what does it mean when considered from a wider point of view? Is there really nothing positive in any of it?

During times of transition from one zodiacal age to another, there is always strife and upheaval. No deep change can take place without some form of death also occurring. If this changeover period coincides with a thorough mess on Earth, the upheavals are inevitably even greater. The arduousness of this particular transition is further intensified by the fact that humanity is now being offered the opportunity of making a quantum leap in consciousness such as has never happened before. The stupendous unrest we are now witnessing is therefore not surprising.

The manner and speed with which the new form of authority emerges on our planet depends entirely on us. Attempting to stem the tide and revert to old patterns, as is being done for instance in Iran, is categorically not the answer. The new young energies will only rise up more violently to counteract such atrophication. It is only with values and ideas appropriate to the New Age that we can start creating, beneath the surface of all the present chaos, the exciting new matrix of authority. Forcibly wrenched from the hands of government, the Church and the army, it is passing already as *inner* authority to each individual according to his capacity.

For the moment we don't know how to handle this. Seeing only pandemonium ahead, we are confused and suspicious. But as each of us starts taking maximum responsibility for ourselves, the anarchical state of the world will slowly subside. When this happens on a practical level, it will also take place in the realm of spiritual authority. As our hearts and minds are filled with the consciousness of the Christ within us, the old Church authority will fade into abeyance.

By their refusal to accept the pre-packed structures bequeathed to them, the postwar generation have begun the process of breaking up the land to receive new seeds. It is now up to all of us to help bring about the marriage of clear minds and compassionate hearts on which will be based the authority of the New Age.

16

Sexuality

One of the areas of greatest change in the coming years will be in our attitude towards sexuality. The Aquarian Age should at last see us attain some of the equilibrium between men and women which has for so long eluded us. It should also be a time when we understand better how closely linked are the sexual and the creative energies, so that in the many circumstances when it is impossible or inappropriate to express our sexuality, these energies can be directed into other forms of creativity.

Since C. G. Jung first postulated the existence of the 'anima' and 'animus', it has become generally recognised that there exist within each man and each woman both the masculine and the feminine principles, and that until both of them are acknowledged and given voice, the individual will not be fully expressed. Although a man will manifest these two principles differently than a woman, their basic characteristics remain the same. The masculine principle is active, outgoing, logical and concerned with making things happen. Its elements are fire and air, representing the dynamic mind qualities. The feminine principle exhibits the complementary characteristics. Its elements are earth and water, which correspond to the receptive emotional qualities. It is passive, intuitive and concerned with the nurturing of that which the male principle has initiated. Both forms of expression are equally necessary; one without the other is a non-event. The more a person can integrate both principles within himself, the more complete will he be, and the less will he work from a position of need – hence weakness.

In all our relationships with people, whether or not they include any sexual expression, we act and react from both our masculine and feminine selves. If a balance exists between these two, a satisfactory state of affairs can be expected: we will be adaptable to the needs of the relationship. When purposefulness and drive are required, we can express those qualities; when gentleness and a listening ear are appropriate, we shift into a more feminine, receptive mode. But where one principle is being over-worked to the detriment of the other, we will be in frequent trouble. By responding always on the same note, we will inevitably be out of tune at least half the time.

A symbol which illustrates this dynamic very well is that of the Essene Tree of Life (see page 79). Standing firm and perfectly in balance, its roots – the feminine side of its nature – delve deep into the ground, drawing from the earth all the sustenance so freely and lovingly given. Its branches – the masculine side of its nature – spring from its trunk Heavenwards, reaching towards God. It is the stability of the roots which allows this exploration to take place; it is the discoveries made by the branches which feed the roots. A creative symbiotic relationship has been established between the two principles. As their complementary energies flow through the tree's trunk, it grows in both height and power.

So should we aim to be, both within ourselves and in our relationships with others: a dual, yet integrated creature, able to act in two modes with equal grace, never confining ourselves to either one lest we grow lop-sided. A painful example of the latter can be seen in strident feminist women. Much of their aggression stems directly from the long repression of the masculine principle in woman and is on that count understandable, even justifiable. But the trouble is that once the repressed principle is given an inch, it grabs a mile and these women become travesties of womankind, more masculine than the most macho man. The new imbalance they have created is as distressing as the previous one.

Wild swings like this one often have to occur before equilibrium can be established, but these fierce Walkyrie women are especially regrettable because they create a sharp polarity with the wimpish

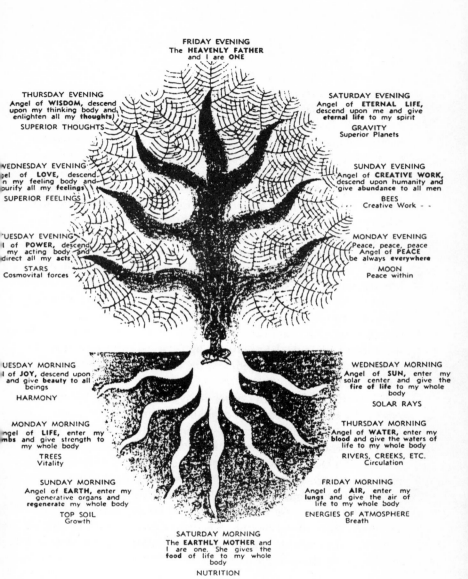

FRIDAY EVENING
The HEAVENLY FATHER
and I are ONE

THURSDAY EVENING
Angel of WISDOM, descend
upon my thinking body and
enlighten all my thoughts
SUPERIOR THOUGHTS

SATURDAY EVENING
Angel of ETERNAL LIFE,
descend upon me and give
eternal life to my spirit
GRAVITY
Superior Planets

WEDNESDAY EVENING
gel of LOVE, descend
n my feeling body and
purify all my feelings
SUPERIOR FEELINGS

SUNDAY EVENING
Angel of CREATIVE WORK,
descend upon humanity and
give abundance to all men
BEES
Creative Work - -

TUESDAY EVENING
l of POWER, descend
my acting body and
direct all my acts
STARS
Cosmovital forces

MONDAY EVENING
Peace, peace, peace
Angel of PEACE
be always everywhere
MOON
Peace within

TUESDAY MORNING
l of JOY, descend upon
and give beauty to all
beings
HARMONY

WEDNESDAY MORNING
Angel of SUN, enter my
solar center and give the
fire of life to my whole
body
SOLAR RAYS

MONDAY MORNING
ngel of LIFE, enter my
mbs and give strength to
my whole body
TREES
Vitality

THURSDAY MORNING
Angel of WATER, enter my
blood and give the waters of
life to my whole body
RIVERS, CREEKS, ETC.
Circulation

SUNDAY MORNING
Angel of EARTH, enter my
generative organs and
regenerate my whole body
TOP SOIL
Growth

FRIDAY MORNING
Angel of AIR, enter my
lungs and give the air of
life to my whole body
ENERGIES OF ATMOSPHERE
Breath

SATURDAY MORNING
The EARTHLY MOTHER and
I are one. She gives the
food of life to my whole
body
NUTRITION

The Essene Tree of Life

men now on the increase. They too are trying desperately to allow their contrasexual natures to be expressed because men's feminine principle, especially in Anglo-Saxon countries, has for years been dealt with as roughly as the masculine principle in women. But many men have not yet found the appropriate means for expressing these unfamiliar energies, and wimpishness is an unfortunate interim stage in their exploration.

The fact that both men and women are suffering at the moment from grave uncertainty about their roles is not really surprising. Not only have the gross imbalances of the past now got to be put right, but we also have to cope with the confusion being caused by a whole range of social changes, such as the increase of one-parent families and working women, the revision of divorce laws and the impact of the West on previously male-oriented cultures.

Jung is reported to have said that in any male/female relationship there are four people present: the man, the woman, the man's anima and the woman's animus. Especially in a relationship which includes sex, it is in the interweaving between these four that the relationship's note is sounded, making it either lasting, ephemeral, damaging or creative.

In a world riddled with pornography, AIDS, child prostitution, rape, child abuse, etc. etc., it is difficult to affirm that the sexual act is a deeply creative one. Yet this statement is true, and one of the most important tasks of the Aquarian Age is to restore sexuality to its proper place, freed of the cruelty and fear, perversions and repressions with which mankind has almost suffocated it.

When shyness and guilt and shame and fear have at last been shaken off so that we can re-possess our sexual nature, then our sacral chakras, seat of all our regenerative powers, will be able to work in harmony with our throat chakras, allowing us greater and greater expressions of creativity.

17

Meditation

Meditation is not a lazy man's euphemism for daydreaming. A true meditative state is extremely positive; from it can emerge not only inner peace, but also a one-pointed state of mind generating great strength and healing power.

Although meditation is usually thought of as originating in the East, contemplation, as practised in the Christian Church, is a close Western equivalent. Both seek the still point where the chattering everyday mind has stilled and inspiration can enter. Popular modern meditation techniques which have been specially adapted for the West, such as Transcendental meditation, tend to emphasise the stress-reducing aspect of meditation, but it can, of course, also be used as it is in the religious life.

The considerable lowering of tension and anxiety in those who meditate regularly has proved to be immensely helpful to many modern followers of this practice, who can now also have the satisfaction of knowing that its efficacy has been proven by electrical machines which measure the various brain patterns: alpha, theta and delta. These machines are also a great help in teaching people how to meditate. When wired to a 'Mind Mirror', various patterns of tiny light bulbs record the level of your brain waves. When an alpha level has been attained through the quietening of your body and mind, you are in the state required for meditation. Identifying the feelings connected with this state helps you to reproduce it at a later date.

There exist of course, both in the East and the West, many

different teachings on meditation. But common to nearly all of them is some form of regular deep breathing. Becoming accustomed during meditation to breathing fully, as few people regularly do, has been a very positive help to better health for many who have carried this practice into their everyday life. More specialized breathing techniques sometimes taught in meditation groups, such as prolonged rapid breathing through the nose, are used for inducing specific states of consciousness and must be practised with discrimination.

The position to be adopted during meditation is of prime importance. This too varies from school to school. Some teach their pupils to sit cross-legged in the 'lotus' position; others kneel on special low wooden stools, and yet others advocate an upright chair. In all cases it is essential that one's back be straight so that energy can be drawn down through all the chakras.

Meditation is an invaluable tool for centering oneself and making contact with the inner or higher worlds. In the hectic atmosphere in which so many of us live, it is often extremely difficult to establish that precious space into which guidance and inspiration can flow. Yet over and over again we are told that this is one of the most important things we can do to help establish peace on earth.

As well as being a pathway into inner peace and contact with higher beings, meditation is a time for more outgoing activities such as 'distant' or 'absent' healing. With the temporary suspension of personality, the putting aside of the ego, we have access to strength and wisdom which we ourselves do not possess. These can in turn be passed on as healing energy for the earth, individuals or groups.

In the West today, meditation teachers are appearing on every corner. Before embarking on a course with any of them, enquire assiduously into what is being offered. If well taught and practised, meditation can be a source of great tranquility and inspiration. If badly taught it is a complete waste of time. Should you consider joining a meditation group, great care should also be exerted. The combined energies of a group can do much to help the world. Equally, strong negative use of a group can be made by an unscrupulous leader. Whatever happens in the group will strongly affect all its members.

18

Religion and Spirituality

The word religion derives from the Latin word *ligere,* to bind. Religion's avowed intent is then to re-bind us to the Godhead. But because most religions have become primarily concerned with temporal and political power, this promise has only too often been interpreted by the Church as the need for constraint. Its followers have not been shown the route to God from whom their spirit could gain strength and joy; they have been deliberately enmeshed in mundane rules and secular matters which kept them firmly under Church control.

It is this intransigent determination to confine people within strict rules, combined with their obsessive desire to 'gain souls' for their particular set of beliefs, that has brought about the totally unjustifiable religious wars and persecutions dogging our history. In the morass of intellectual arguments and fighting, the fundamental justification for religion has only too often sunk without trace. Divorced from spirituality, which should be its very essence, the Church has become in many cases an empty shell.

Excessive dogma has the added disavantage of throwing people primarily into their minds, making a direct linking of the individual with God almost impossible as this must stem from the heart. It is in those religious sects which sought to have a minimum of dogma, such as the Quakers, where these direct links have most consistently been formed.

As a result of this sad state of affairs, few people know themselves as integral droplets of the Divine, whose entire lives could be a song of joy to this unity. By decreeing that all contact with God must go through them, most priesthoods have deliberately created a gulf between God and his people. The ropes of faith have been used to bind men to the Church rather than to God. Fear of punishment and promises of salvation have been mercilessly used to maintain this status quo.

It was the Protestant affirmation that man could know and serve God without the intercession of priests or saints which made the tightly-knotted ropes of Christianity begin to creak. In the Aquarian Age we must go yet further so that the promises of Jesus can become a reality. By making ourselves truly self-responsible and reliably guided by our Higher Selves, we will know God to be in us and we in Him at all times and in all places. When we can find Him as readily in a prison cell or at the kitchen sink as we can in Chartres Cathedral, no outside power will be able to stand between Him and us.

An important step in bringing about this shift in responsibility is to draw up new guidelines for our children. To have them blindly memorizing prayers and performing rituals which have often lost their meaning, will do nothing to help them towards this total identification with God. It will only swell the vast ranks of those who defect from the teachings of their childhood, or simply let them slip into abeyance. Having been vaccinated by religion, they become immune to spirituality. These questions can no longer be left to chance. We must help them understand from an early age that spirituality is not just for Sunday mornings. It is for all day every day; there is no separation between matters of the spirit and the material world since spirit is everywhere.

If it is true that we arrive on earth 'trailing clouds of glory', awareness of the reality of God in everything and everyone is a natural condition. If we can help our children retain it, for them He will always be 'closer than breathing'. The Christ child can be born in their hearts.

19

Health and Disease

Disease is not such a disaster as modern Western thinking has led us to believe. Nor is it without its value. Nor are we its victims: most disease is self-generated, the direct result of some process we have set in motion during this or a former lifetime.

In direct contrast to the equally drastic attitude of the East, where ill-health is fatalistically accepted, we in the West are taught to strive for the maximum good health possible to us. It is even optimistically hoped that the great advances in scientific and medical knowledge will one day eliminate disease. Such hope, born of material and escapist thinking, conceives of our bodies as mechanical objects which can be mended, and, if necessary, improved upon.

But our bodies are not just an assemblage of spare parts whose good working we can guarantee through regular overhauls. Their smooth running does not depend solely on such controllable factors as good feeding, proper rest and protection from contagious disease. To deny the existence of the psyche and spirit, which influence the body every moment of the day and night, is patently unreasonable. How often does a medical examination disclose no anomalies, yet the patient feels very ill, whereas someone dying in great pain can be feeling no concern for his body, because his mind and soul are so at peace.

The assumption that death is the ultimate failure of health and healing is another major misconception which is in direct contrast with the attitude of the East. There they accept the spiritual teaching that we will die at an appointed time. Just as we choose our moment of entry onto the planet, so have we chosen our time for leaving it. No amount of organ transplants, drugs, resuscitation or spiritual healing can alter this, they say. For them it is not only impossible to prolong our lives beyond their allotted span, it is also undesirable to try, because it diverts our attention from where it should be – on our death.

Our dying is as important as our living; it is the summation of all we have been and learned in this lifetime. To die cravenly, clutching desperately at earth life prevents us from completing this cycle peacefully. Although the pain and sorrow of dying may well be very difficult to endure, especially if we are leaving loved ones behind, death itself cannot be regarded as frightening once we accept it as an adventure we have already undertaken many times. Nor can we feel in any way cheated when we have realized that there is no such thing as an untimely death. As a vital element in our view of health and disease, our dying must not be tucked under the carpet until that moment when it forces itself upon our attention. Only in this way can it be deprived of its potential power to shatter our dignity and serenity just when we most need them.

For anyone who views life on earth as a learning process, disease can be seen as a very fruitful teacher, at times the only one to whom we would be willing to listen. Like an accident, it tends to focus our attention on that which needs to be addressed and has been avoided. When seeking to interpret the messages being given by a particular disease, it is important to consider both its nature and its site in our body. An affliction of the lungs, for instance, could indicate that we are not drawing into our being the spirit (air) we need. A chronic throat infection would almost certainly be pinpointing our attention on that chakra through which many forms of creativity should be expressing themselves. As we become more alert to this language of the body, we can learn much about ourselves that our conscious minds could never reveal. If, however, we persist in blocking out these messages of distress, the disease into which they have been translated will become more persistent. It can eventually narrow our lives to a hospital bed, from which it will be exceedingly difficult not to face what we have been so strenuously avoiding.

All self-destructive activities such as drug-taking and alcoholism can be seen as the same mechanism unconsciously at work. But here impatience has intervened in the process: the addict is wilfully provoking a crisis in order to force a response from himself. The danger is that he might blow apart his own receiving station so that the messages he is so impatiently requesting cannot be captured. Instead of accelerating his growth, he will have severely curtailed it. Expert help will almost certainly be needed in order to reconstruct what has been destroyed.

If each of our lives is a bead upon a necklace rather than an isolated event, it is easy to conceive of certain diseases being direct carry-overs from the past. Out of the extensive investigations on this fascinating subject done by the great American seer, Edgar Cayce, two basic facts emerge: the first is that if we inflict harm on someone, we often undergo the same physical or emotional pain ourselves in a later life so as to understand and redeem what we have done. Cayce's second finding was that the intensity of the retribution required depends largely on the degree of consciousness and self-responsibility accompanying the action in the past.

A second category of painful carry-over conditions stems from violent occurrences or deaths which were either so rapid, unexpected, or intensely painful that they were not properly processed at the time. Some physical reminder of that former happening is needed by the present personality in order for him to integrate it into his total life's experience.

The past-life recall of a young man who was floundering in search of his path illustrates several aspects of these phenomena. In re-connecting with his life as a Franciscan monk in the 16th century, he found that the Spanish Inquisition had broken his back then in exactly the same places where it was now badly damaged since birth. On leaving the Spanish prison, completely bent over as he would be for the rest of that lifetime, the monk turned, and with a smile of great tenderness held out to the present-day incarnation of himself a quill pen.

When the recall had ended, the young man knew without any doubt that he had, in several incarnations, often in great danger, been a recorder of the esoteric wisdom. By accepting the monk's proffered pen, his path became totally clear to him. And his back, though no less painful, became an active teacher and instrument for redemption instead of a resented affliction. His realization that it was his root and heart chakras that were damaged in both lives was also a great help. He could now see that the lessons he had set up for himself through his choice of present-day circumstances centred around those two areas. Knowing this he was able to work psychologically and spiritually in a far more intense and specific way. As the past life recall gradually became absorbed into his psyche, many more insights emerged, including much teaching on forgiveness, a central theme in his life from then on. How beautifully and economically had the Higher World used an apparently destructive physical imperfection.

Once we begin to recognize some of the complicated ramifications of health and disease, and have acknowledged that our bodies as well as our souls are intimately linked with past lives, we will take a quite different view of those to whom we are willing to confide our well-being.

Preventive medicine is already assuming a far more prominent role in modern life. And not only physically: New Age therapists are making their clients increasingly aware of how certain mental sets can encourage certain diseases. Increased attention to diet and exercise, and the practice of yoga, meditation, the martial arts, massage and many stress-relieving therapies, are also helping to prevent much suffering. Eventually our health services may even be able to run on the satisfactory Chinese principle that doctors are paid only when their patients do not need them.

Any practitioner who sees his patient as a composite of which one piece can be treated without regard for the whole, cannot qualify as giving adequate care. Even the most highly specialized medical technicians must begin to see themselves as part of a team looking after a *human being*. In the atmosphere of high-tech modern hospitals, this fact sometimes gets sadly submerged. Modern allopathic medicine has made breath-taking advances in alleviating man's diseases, but in the process much has been lost. It is to be hoped that with the growth of complementary medicine and co-operation between the two, a more holistic treatment of the patient will gradually develop.

The range of 'complementary' therapies is wide and growing all the time. Great care and discrimination is needed in choosing a therapist because there are without doubt many unscrupulous and ill-trained ones about. Yet slowly the credentials required of the members of these therapeutic associations are becoming more stringent, and as a result they are gaining more credence both from the public and the establishment. Referrals to healers, acupuncturists and other alternative practitioners are increasing all the time. More and more people are also realizing that it is in the combining of conventional medicine with complementary medicine that our hope lies. To cut ourselves off from either is a terrible waste.

As the co-operation between our spirit, mind and body grows, we will intuitively know where to seek help. It could be from a spiritual teacher, a psychotherapist or a medical doctor, an acupuncturist, an osteopath, a masseur, or even a combination of two or three of these. Above all we must learn to care for all levels of our being, not just the physical.

20

Accidents and Coincidences

According to the Aquarian world-view, nothing in our life happens by chance, even so-called accidents. Neither the result of coincidence nor bad luck, they are seen as part of a pattern serving in different ways to help us towards spiritual awareness and wholeness.

Once we can endorse the reality of reincarnation and acknowledge the vast pattern to which we belong as individuals, members of a group, and citizens of a nation and planet, it is easier to accept the premise that things are happening to us, and we are precipitating events, which are necessary to the over-all design. If we can relinquish the need and desire to understand the details of this complex pattern and simply contribute to it, our life becomes relatively manageable: we can flow with it, never feeling isolated, yet also not feeling harrassed or drained by all those unknown strands with which we are so intimately interlinked. Whatever presents itself to us requires our full attention. That is the best we can promise to give.

In this spirit of active acceptance, and in order to pursue further the concept of an individual pattern integrally part of a global one, let us return to the idea that we ourselves choose the detailed circumstances of our lives. When making those choices we had an overall view of both this incarnation and of the sum total of all our lives; they were made by our own soul in conjunction with beings whose wisdom and love are unequivocal. Those choices then can be trusted. We must not doubt them simply because our overall

vision becomes clouded at birth. None of the choices were accidental or frivolous. Each of them, whether it be the identity of our
parents, the constitution of our physical body, or the nature of our
marriage, was there to provide us with the challenge or support
needed in this lifetime.

The spiritual law of economy requires that nothing in life be
wasted. So if the building blocks given to us at birth are not being
used, we must have wandered off our path, or at least fallen asleep
under a tree somewhere along the way. As time also is not to be
wasted, the Higher Worlds will probably at this point give us a
nudge to get us back onto that path. The first of these will be quite
gentle, especially if we are not yet in contact with our Higher Self
and have no clear idea of where we are going. A dream, an intuitive
flash, a 'chance' meeting, or a book which 'happens' to come our
way, may well do the trick. Our attention having been drawn to the
lacunae or inconsistencies in our life, we move off again in the right
direction.

But we may of course refuse the nudge. If this is the case, nothing
will be done to interfere with our free will. We will simply be
making it more difficult for ourselves. And we will be setting up a
conflict between our personal life and that of the greater pattern we
had agreed to serve. It is when this conflict becomes too marked
that further action must be taken by our guides and helpers. Because
although we must be allowed to wreck our own life if we want to,
there comes a point when the overall pattern must be given priority.
If too heavy an imbalance has been created and is ruining the
effectiveness of too many people, a sharper nudge will be admini-
stered.

Remaining impervious to this one will be more difficult. The
recurring dream that awakens us night after night will be more
disturbing. The coming together of several synchronistic events will
be so powerful that even the strongest scepticism, or desire to
disregard them, will not be able to conceal their existence. Should
we still refuse to take any action, an 'accident', or even a series of
them, will be resorted to.

The messages these accidents impart will be as specific as those given through disease. If they are to be truly understood and acted upon, every detail of the event should be carefully considered. Was it commenting, for instance, on our way of journeying through life (a car, train or plane accident)? Or was it concerned with our psychic space (a fire or theft in our house)? Was it about the masculine or feminine principles within us (which side of our body has been hurt)? Have we been temporarily or permanently incapacitated in order that we use our energies more purposefully? Must we learn from this happening what it is like to be in some way dependent on others?

That part of our body which was involved in the accident will also provide clues. As each of our limbs and organs is connected to a different sign of the Zodiac and a different element (earth, air, fire and water), having a heart attack, for instance, is a fiery Leo event, concentrating us on all that is related to our intuition and its expression. An injury to a leg is asking for a re-assessment of the foundations on which we have built our life. A damaged sense organ is commenting on the way we apprehend life, specifically through that organ.

Although it may seem incredible to maintain that accidents on a larger scale – seemingly haphazard events such as motorway pile-ups, nuclear leakages, volcanic eruptions or the collapse of a bridge – could possibly form part of a plan to further our spiritual journey, the justification for such an allegation seems to lie in the law of karma and the law of attraction. According to the former, the apparent 'victims' of these disasters would in fact, in the most economical way possible, be working out events from their specific soul history through the accident. According to the law of attraction, each of us draws to himself what he needs, whether it be a terrifying experience, or the chance to perform an act of heroism. As with personal accidents, if the message given through the disaster is acknowledged and consciously absorbed into the person's life, there will be no further need for 'accidents' or untoward 'coincidences'.

Our greatest difficulty in accepting accidents as nudges – or indeed sledgehammer blows – from above stems from our human perspective. Unable to see the whole, we cannot appreciate the infinite complexity of this pattern being worked out and the need for certain events. But if willing to take this idea on faith, our reaction to accidents as an attack provoking resentment and bitterness will fade. We will be able to see them as clues on our path. Instead of crashing through life seeing and hearing nothing but our own footsteps, we will begin to follow our trail like a Red Indian, alert to every bent twig and displaced stone.

21

Recall of Past Lives

There are two reasons why an increasing number of people are now beginning to remember their past lives. First of all the present climate is far more open and accepting than it has been for a very long time. Secondly, modern regression techniques have improved, and more therapists are using them. Through the knowledge gained in this way, people's belief in reincarnation has been greatly strengthened, and its workings have become better understood. There are, however, undoubtedly dangers involved in both induced and spontaneous past-life recall of which we should be aware.

Out of the great variety of experiences we have undergone in the past, what we need to remember for this particular lifetime will be very specific. Any induced recall should then be prefaced by the request that we see what is right and relevant for now, and no more. Only in this way can we be sure that the right memories surface. In the case of spontaneous recalls, they are likely to be appropriate or they would not have happened.

That total psychic trust must exist between the therapist and the person being regressed (taken into a past life), goes without saying. Only someone of the highest integrity, discretion and knowledge should be entrusted with this task. In varying degrees of clarity and intensity, scenes and emotions from some former lifetime are going to be re-experienced, and although the situations can be happy or interesting, they can also be unpleasant or even distressing. Considerable psychological training and spiritual insight are therefore needed on the part of the therapist in order that the regression be a creative experience.

As important as one's choice of regressor, is one's motivation for doing this work. If it is superficial curiosity or a need for self-aggrandizement, forget it. We are being offered this knowledge from the past for a very specific reason: to give us greater understanding of situations and relationships which have been carried over into our present lifetime. Psychic protection will be afforded to those who approach regression with this in mind. Those who come to it in a mood of frivolity or sensation seeking must not expect this protection, and may well experience difficulties beyond those naturally inherent in regressions.

If, however, optimum conditions can be established, and the client has defined with maximum clarity his queries, a wide range of helpful information can emerge out of past life recalls. If, for instance, someone found that he had been consistently following the path of the priest-healer in all his lives, this could be very helpful in establishing his present direction and strengths. He could also possibly contact some of his former knowledge and skills so that they be brought forward for use now.

Another very useful fact that is sometimes established through recalls, is the location of our spiritual home. That is the place where we first incarnated and aligned ourselves with certain tasks and basic qualities which will remain with us throughout all our incarnations. It would seem that we return there from time to time in order to re-affirm that particular spiritual commitment and way of expressing ourselves. For those who are now incarnate in a Western Christian society but have that original spiritual home in some quite different part of the planet, discovering its whereabouts can bring security at a very deep level, and also ban the loneliness they feel in their present 'alien' surroundings.

One of the most common incentives for attempting a regression is a wish to know our past connections with someone we have rediscovered in this lifetime. Again motive is all-important. If the research is undertaken out of idle curiosity or in order to gain power over someone, no good will come of it. But if the relationship with that person seems to be a significant factor in our karmic task, then it could be very helpful to establish several basic facts about it. Are we, for instance, members of the same soul group? If so, we can expect from the relationship a very special quality: extremely demanding yet at the same time very supportive. It could also be useful to know whether we have spent lives as members of the same family, and if so, in what relationship and how successful were they? What karmic debts between us need to be redeemed? Were our relationships in past lives based on trust and love or did envy and jealousy also play their part?

For someone who does not want to enter into a regression himself, there are also now many psychics able to give a 'reading' of past lives. Using a signature or an habitually worn object as a 'witness', they can 'tune in', sometimes in great detail, to lives in which we have participated. Certain astrologers can also deduce much information about past lives from a birth chart. It is often through one of these that newcomers first explore their past. But great care must be taken here. It is so easy to be gullible and be exploited. This is especially true if our wishful thinking is being satisfied: by being told, for instance, that we were once some important historical character – as seems to happen suspiciously often. These declarations, made in the circumstances they are, can carry a lot of weight. Their glamour and seductiveness must not be allowed to complicate our lives. There are bad regressors and psychics like there are bad members of any profession, and if we just accept unquestioningly what they tell us, we can be in real trouble. Any connections with past lives that we need to know this time around will, after careful scrutiny, feel right. The others must be dropped.

Another circumstance in which past-life information can prove very disturbing and confusing is when the client does not request any specific information but simply accepts whatever comes through the psychic, as is common practice with many 'readings' by post. In the likely event of this information being irrelevant to his current explorations, he will be unable to relate to the images evoked. They are then reduced to being interesting pieces of cinema rather than constructive elements in the jigsaw puzzle of his spiritual evolution.

The other real danger from these 'readings' can lie in the nature of the images or incidents brought forward. They can be really over-whelming. If someone totally identifies with that former personality, and takes on its guilts or sadnesses, he can be in grave trouble. To approach past lives in this non-discriminating way is like 'forcing' a plant so violently that you cause it to wilt; it takes some considerable time before balanced growth can resume.

There is another potentially harmful factor in a recall done via a psychic instead of being personally experienced. Because it is received at an intellectual rather than a gut level, the images and emotions are less real, and can more easily be edited. This can be dangerous. If genuine, the image was given to us in order that it be dealt with – *not* for it to be denied and rejected because it conflicts with our self-image. We are then left with only the interesting, exciting, or even flattering parts of the recall, which of course feeds one of the worst scourges of the New Age: self-inflation. Although it can well be argued that it is our more passionate, active lives which are most deeply impressed on our past life record, and are therefore more easily recalled, everyone must at some times have experienced humble, consolidating lives. Those too must be taken into account.

Whether we are experiencing induced or spontaneous recalls, or ones given to us by a psychic, it is wise to have someone of considerable experience in these matters to whom we can turn in case of difficulty. The images and their implications will not always be easy to assimilate, and it is of paramount importance that someone be able to help us put things into perspective.

If knowledge of the past is really part of your development for this lifetime, approach it at a pace you can endure, prepared to assimilate whatever is presented to you, good or bad, grand or humble. It is from the agglomerate of all these that understanding and compassion can be reached, and a framework built on which to hang all the new discoveries of this lifetime, making them a living creative part of your totality. Used wisely, and if right for you, past-life recall can be one of the most effective tools for raising consciousness and helping you become part of a whole new perspective.

22

Free Will

To most people the concept of predestination is anathema. No one wants to be robbed of his freedom and power by being told that he must blindly follow a set of tramlines laid down for him at birth. Nor does he want to feel irrevocably trapped into a certain mode of behaviour dictated by the personality and background with which he was endowed.

Free will is a cornerstone of New Age thinking. Although each of us is integrally part of the divine plan for the Universe, that basic structure onto which everything hangs and without which nothing could work, our behaviour and our growth-rate within that plan are entirely up to us. The life given to us at birth is not an arbitrary one. It represents the sum total of all our lives to date. Having exerted free will between lives to chose its broad outlines – we can continue to exert it now through our handling of those conditions.

One of the promises of the Aquarian Age is that the scope of our free will be increased to the limit of what each of us can handle. Only in this way can human beings take that step towards their potential which is one of the main tasks of the coming age. Until now, our range of choice has been limited. Nearly all of us had to belong to some kind of group in order to have our behaviour defined for us. We had to follow those who declared their wisdom – genuinely or fraudulently – to be greater than ours. But the Aquarian individual will responsibly assume the power and strength to run his own life in accordance with a far more direct perception of what that life should be. This does not mean that society will lack all structures. It means that each individual will have far more say in the role he plays. As aspiring co-creators with God, we will actually form new conditions of life on Earth instead of accepting the predominantly disastrous ones which have accumulated over the years.

It is extremely important that we now loudly declare the reality of free will. Nearly everything in our modern computerized society works to make us feel that we are infinitesimally minute cogs in a machine so gigantic and uncaring that there is no way we can take charge of our own lives. When an electricity strike occurs, for instance, there is absolutely nothing we can do about it, except to pursue our life with a candle in one hand. However much we may deplore a government policy decision on education, we still have to send our children to school, because such is the law of the land. In instances like these it is difficult to talk about free will, which seems to serve us less and less. Yet, nevertheless, we must not lose faith in it.

Another discouraging thing at the moment is the way in which free will is manifesting itself. However stultifying total obedience and conformism can be, they seem at times almost preferable to that misguided use of free will which flouts all established convention and results in disastrous anti-social behaviour, ranging from football hooliganism to the worst sexual excesses. But if we can understand this rebelliousness as a reaction to the ant-like quality of contemporary life, we see that it has scant connection with the eventual use of free will by Aquarian man. In tune with his Higher Self, and beginning to understand the true purpose of his life, his thoughts and actions will come to flow in line with that purpose. Whatever the outer circumstances confronting him, they will be accepted and used as tools for progress.

A good way to envisage the use of free will within the parameters given to us, is to imagine life as a journey. If we board our train in London with Inverness as our destination, we cannot suddenly decide to change onto the line to Bristol, or opt for an airplane instead of the railway; no basic facts which existed in London (female, Caucasian, Cancerian, etc.) can be altered in mid-journey.

But within those parameters, our choice of behaviour is total. We could hire an entire carriage and sleep all the way to Scotland. We could drive everyone crackers by pounding a drum up and down the corridor. We could set fire to the seats and smash all the buffet crockery. We could set ourselves up as the first aid station for the entire train. We could even dress up as a clown and provide entertainment for all the children. The possibilities are infinite. Within the set limits, our free will has total liberty. And by one of those strange paradoxes of spiritual law, the more we behave in accordance with the law, the freer we become.

Afterword

We are not mere grains of sand on a dreary beach, nor are we dead numbers in the social security archives. We are not nuclear bomb fodder, nor the puppets of governing bodies. We are droplets of the Divine, potential co-creators with God. Everything we do, every thought we think, is of the utmost importance. Our potential is a thousand times greater than we have ever been led to believe. As we move into the New Age, let us take heart and courage. Good will prevail "All will be well, all will be infinitely well", as was asserted by Julian of Norwich so many years ago.

Reading List

Chapter 1
Eastcott, Michal: *Entering Aquarius*, Sundial House
Stanley-Alder, Vera: *Initiation of the World*, Rider, 1968
Reid, Vera: *Towards Aquarius*, Rider 1971

Chapter 2
Germinara, Gina: *Many Mansions*, Spearman 1967
Cayce, Edgar: *On Reincarnation*, Warner Books (USA)
Challoner, H. K.: *Wheel of Rebirth* Theosophical 1969
Grant, Joan: *Winged Pharoah*, Sphere 1973

Chapter 3
Besant, Annie: *Karma*, Theosophical

Chapter 4
Powell, A. E.: *The Etheric Double*, Theosophical 1979
Bek, Lila & Pullar, Phillipa: *Seven Levels of Healing*, Century 1986
Tansley, David: *Raiment of Light*, Penguin

Chapter 5
St Aubyn, Lorna: *Healing*, Heinemann 1983
Young, Alan: *Spiritual Healing*, DeVorss 1982
Pullar, Philippa: *Spiritual and Lay Healing*, Penguin
Taylor, Allegra: *I Fly out with Bright Feathers*, Fontana

Chapter 6
Michell, John: *View over Atlantis*, Abacus 1975
Graves, Tom: *Needles of Stone*, Turnstone (Gothic Image) 1986
Cooke, Grace: *The Light in Britain*, White Eagle 1971
Fidler, J. H.: *Earth Energies*, Turnstone (Thorsons) 1983
Noyes, Ralph (ed): *The Crop Circle Enigma,* Gateway 1990

Chapter 7
White, Ruth: *A Question of Guidance*, C. W. Daniel 1989
Dean, Michael (ed.): *The Guide Book*, Gateway Books 1986
White Eagle: *Mediumship*

Chapter 8
Russell, Peter: *The Awakening Earth*, Ark 1984
Schumacher, E. F.: *Small is Beautiful*, Sphere 1974
Sheldrake, Rupert: *A New Science of Life*, A. Blond 1985
Watson, Lyall: *Supernature I + II*, Hodder 1973

Chapter 9
Levine, Stephen: *Meetings at the Edge*, Anchor Press (Ashgrove)
Krystal, Phyllis: *Cutting the Ties that Bind*, Turnstone (Element) 1980
Kubler-Ross, Elisabeth: *Living with Death and Dying*, Souvenir 1982
Dass, Ram & Gordon, Paul: *How can I help?*, Century 1986
Greaves, Helen: *Testimony of Light*, C. W. Daniel 1969
"Visions of Hope". video, Michaelmas Trust

Chapter 10
Jampolsky: *Love is letting go of fear*, Celestial Arts 1985
White, Ruth & Sainson, Mary: *The Healing Spectrum*, C. W. Daniel 1979
Scott-Peck, M.: *The Road Less Travelled*, Century 1987

Chapter 11
Kubler-Ross, Elisabeth: *On death and dying*, Routledge 1973
Moody, Raymond: *Life after Life*, Corgi-Bantam 1977
Watson, Lyall: *The Romeo Error*, Hodder 1974
Beard, Paul: *Survival of Death*, Pilgrims Book Serv. 1983

Chapter 12
Liedloff, Jean: *Continuum Concept*, Futura 1976
Vissell, Barry & Joyce: *The Shared Heart*, Ramira 1984
Salter, Joan: *The Incarnating Child*, Hawthorne Press (USA)
Wickes, Frances: *The Inner World of Childhood*, Coventure (Element)
   1977

Chapter 13
Bailey, Alice: *Education in the New Age*, Lucis Press 1971
Whitmore, Diana: *Psychosynthesis in Education*, Turnstone (Thorsons)
   1986

Chapter 14
Greene, Liz & Sasportas, Howard: *The Development of Personality*,
   Penguin 1989
Ferrucci, Piero: *What We May Be*, Turnstone (Thorsons) 1982

Chapter 15
Golen, Thadeus: *A lazy man's guide to Enlightenment*, Bantam (USA)
Keyes, Ken: *Handbook to Higher Consciousness*, Living Love (USA)
   1985
Rogers, Carl: *On personal power*, Constable 1978

Chapter 16
Cayce, Edgar: *Sex and the Spiritual Path*, A. R. E. Press (USA)
Harding, Esther: *Women's Mysteries*, Rider
Bailey, Alice: *Compilation on Sex*, Lucis Press
Singer, June: *Androgyny*, Routledge 1977
Miller, Stuart: *Men and Friendship*, Gateway Books 1983
Johnson, R. A.: *The Psychology of Romantic Love*, Penguin

Chapter 17
Eastcott, Michal: *The Silent Path*, Rider 1969
LeShan, Lawrence: *How to Meditate*, Turnstone (Thorsons) 1983
Cooke, Grace: *Meditation*, White Eagle 1955

Chapter 18
Banks, Natalie: *The Golden Thread*, Lucis Press 1967
Johnston, William: *Silent Music*, Fountana 1976
Freedom Long, Max: *The Secret Science Behind Miracles*, DeVorss
Trevelyan, George: *Operation Redemption*, Stillpoint (Gateway) 1981
Tudor Pole, Wesley & Lehmann, Rosamund: *My dear Alexia*, Spearman
   1979

Chapter 19
Hay, Louise: *You Can Heal Your Life*, Eden Grove 1987
LeShan, Lawrence: *Holistic Health,* Turnstone (Thorsons) 1984

Chapter 20
Greene, Liz: *Astrology of Fate*, Unwin Mandala 1985
Rogers, Carl: *On becoming a person*, Constable 1974

Chapter 21
Glaskin, G. M.: *Windows of the Mind*, Wildwood House 1974

Resources

PSYCHIC ADVICE
College of Psychic Studies
16 Queensbury Place, London S W 7
Tel: 071 589 3292

THERAPISTS
Institute for Transpersonal Psychology
7 Pembridge Place
London W2

Psychosynthesis and Education Trust
188 Old Street, London EC1V 9BP
Tel: 071 636 9543

Institute for Complementary Medicine
21 Portland Place, London W 1.
Tel: 071 636 9543

HEALING SCHOOLS
Le Plan International School of Healing
Le Petit Canadeau, Le Plan du Castellet,
Le Beausset, Var, 83330, France
Tel: 01033 949 87241

College of Healing
Runnings Park, Croft Bank, West Malvern,
Worcs WR14 4BP
Tel: 06845 65290